Mastering Culinary Delights: A Beginner's Guide to Cooking

By Gigi Diab

Mastering Culinary Delights: A Beginner's Guide to Cooking

By Gigi Diab

MASTERING CULINARY DELIGHTS: A BEGINNER'S GUIDE TO COOKING

First edition. June 30, 2024.

ISBN: 979-8227494047

Written by Gigi Diab.

Chapter 1: Introduction to Cooking

Why Learn To Cook?

Learning to cook offers a multitude of benefits that can enhance various aspects of your life. Here are some compelling reasons why learning to cook is worthwhile:

1. **Healthier Eating**: Cooking your own meals allows you to have full control over the ingredients, enabling you to make healthier choices. You can reduce sodium, sugar, and unhealthy fats, and increase the use of nutritious ingredients like vegetables, lean proteins, and whole grains.

2. **Cost Savings**: Eating out or ordering takeout regularly can be expensive. Cooking at home is generally more economical, as you can buy ingredients in bulk, use leftovers creatively, and avoid service charges and tips.

3. **Creativity and Personal Satisfaction**: Cooking is a creative outlet where you can experiment with flavors, textures, and cuisines. Creating a dish from scratch and seeing others enjoy it can be incredibly satisfying.

4. **Bonding with Others**: Cooking can be a social activity that brings people together. Whether you're cooking with family, friends, or your partner, it provides an opportunity for bonding and creating lasting memories.

5. **Independence and Self-Sufficiency**: Knowing how to cook means you're less reliant on others for your meals. It empowers you to take care of yourself and others, whether you're living alone or with others.

6. **Cultural Appreciation**: Cooking allows you to explore different cultures through their cuisines. Trying new recipes from around the world can broaden your culinary horizons and deepen your understanding of diverse traditions.

7. **Stress Relief**: Engaging in cooking can be a therapeutic activity, helping you to unwind and focus on a task that requires your full attention. It can serve as a form of mindfulness and relaxation.

8. **Life Skill**: Cooking is a practical life skill that you can use daily. It's not just about following recipes but also understanding ingredients, techniques, and flavors, which can be applied in various aspects of your life.

9. **Impressing Others**: Being able to cook well can impress guests at dinner parties or gatherings. It's a skill that often garners admiration and appreciation from others.

10. **Adaptability and Problem-Solving**: Cooking teaches you to think on your feet and improvise when necessary. You learn to work with what you have, troubleshoot issues, and adjust recipes to suit your taste or dietary needs.

In essence, learning to cook is about more than just preparing meals—it's about nurturing yourself and others, exploring creativity, and gaining valuable life skills that contribute to a healthier, more fulfilling lifestyle.

Overcoming Common Myths About Cooking

Cooking can sometimes seem intimidating or fraught with misconceptions that deter people from trying it. Here are some common myths about cooking and how to overcome them:

Myth: Cooking is difficult and requires special talent.

Reality: Cooking is a skill that anyone can learn with practice and patience. Start with simple recipes and gradually build your confidence. There are plenty of beginner-friendly resources like cookbooks, online tutorials, and cooking classes to help you get started.

Myth: You need fancy equipment and expensive ingredients to cook well.

Reality: While high-quality equipment can enhance your cooking experience, you don't need a fully stocked chef's kitchen to make delicious meals. Many dishes can be prepared with basic kitchen tools like knives, pots, and pans. Simple, fresh ingredients often yield the best results, and budget-friendly options can be just as tasty.

Myth: Cooking takes too much time.

Reality: Not all meals require hours of preparation. There are plenty of quick and easy recipes that can be whipped up in 30 minutes or less. With meal planning and efficient cooking techniques, you can streamline your kitchen time and still enjoy homemade meals.

Myth: You have to follow recipes exactly or they won't turn out right.

Reality: Recipes are guidelines, not strict rules. Feel free to adjust ingredients based on your preferences or what you have on hand. Cooking is about creativity and experimentation. As you gain experience, you'll develop a sense of intuition about flavors and techniques.

Myth: Cooking is messy and cleanup is a hassle.

Reality: Cooking can be organized and efficient with a bit of planning. Keep your workspace tidy as you work, and clean as you go to minimize the post-cooking cleanup. Using fewer utensils and bowls by multitasking with them can also make cleanup easier.

Myth: Only professional chefs can create restaurant-quality meals.

Reality: Many restaurant-quality dishes are actually based on simple cooking techniques and quality ingredients. With practice and attention to detail, you can replicate delicious flavors at home. Remember, presentation and flavor balance are key components of a great dish.

Myth: You have to be a natural-born cook to enjoy cooking.

Reality: Cooking can be enjoyable for anyone, regardless of initial skill level. It's a skill that improves with practice, and the satisfaction of creating something delicious can be deeply rewarding. Start with dishes you love or cuisines you're curious about to keep your motivation high.

By challenging these myths and approaching cooking with a positive mindset, you can cultivate a fulfilling and enjoyable culinary experience. Experiment, learn from mistakes, and celebrate your successes—it's all part of the journey towards becoming a confident home cook.

Essential Tools and Equipment

Having the right tools and equipment is essential for a smooth and enjoyable cooking experience. Here's a list of some basic kitchen tools and equipment that every home cook should have:

Chef's Knife: A good-quality chef's knife is the cornerstone of any kitchen. It should be sharp, comfortable to hold, and capable of slicing, dicing, and chopping various ingredients.

Cutting Board: Choose a sturdy cutting board made from wood or plastic. It should be large enough to comfortably chop vegetables, meat, and other ingredients without overcrowding.

Pots and Pans: Invest in a few versatile pots and pans, such as a medium-sized saucepan, a large skillet or frying pan, and a stockpot for boiling pasta or making soups.

Baking Sheets and Ovenware: Baking sheets are useful for roasting vegetables, baking cookies, or making sheet pan meals. Oven-safe dishes like casserole dishes or roasting pans are also handy for preparing larger meals.

Mixing Bowls: Have a set of mixing bowls in various sizes for combining ingredients, marinating meats, mixing salads, or serving dishes.

Measuring Cups and Spoons: Accurate measuring is crucial in cooking. Have both dry measuring cups (for flour, sugar, etc.) and liquid measuring cups (for liquids like water or oil). Measuring spoons are also essential for precise measurements of smaller quantities.

Utensils: Stock your kitchen with essential utensils such as a spatula, slotted spoon, wooden spoons, tongs, whisk, ladle, and a pasta server. Silicone or heat-resistant utensils are great for use with non-stick cookware.

Kitchen Scale: A kitchen scale is useful for measuring ingredients by weight, which can be more accurate than measuring by volume, especially for baking.

Colander/Strainer: Essential for draining pasta, rinsing vegetables, and straining liquids.

Can Opener: A sturdy can opener is essential for opening canned goods and ingredients.

Kitchen Timer: Whether it's a separate timer or a timer on your phone, having a reliable way to keep track of cooking times is crucial.

Grater/Zester: Useful for grating cheese, zesting citrus fruits, and grating spices like nutmeg or ginger.

Kitchen Towels and Oven Mitts: Keep several kitchen towels handy for drying hands, wiping spills, and handling hot dishes. Oven mitts or heat-resistant gloves are essential for safely handling hot pots and pans.

Small Appliances: Depending on your cooking preferences, consider adding small appliances like a blender, food processor, stand mixer, or immersion blender for tasks such as blending sauces, mixing dough, or pureeing soups.

Storage Containers: Have a variety of food storage containers for storing leftovers, prepped ingredients, and pantry staples.

By equipping your kitchen with these basic tools and equipment, you'll have everything you need to tackle a wide range of recipes and cooking techniques with confidence. As you gain experience and refine your cooking skills, you may choose to expand your collection with specialized tools or gadgets that suit your cooking style.

Chapter 2: Getting Started in the Kitchen

Setting Up Your Kitchen Space

Setting up your kitchen space for cooking efficiently and comfortably is essential for enjoying your culinary endeavors. Here's a step-by-step guide to help you set up your kitchen space effectively:

Step 1: Declutter and Clean

Before setting up your kitchen for cooking, start with a clean slate:

Clear out unnecessary items: Remove items that you rarely use or that don't belong in the kitchen.

Clean surfaces: Wipe down countertops, shelves, and cabinets to create a clean and inviting workspace.

Step 2: Organize Your Kitchen Layout

Consider the layout of your kitchen and organize it for maximum efficiency:

Work Triangle: Arrange your stove, sink, and refrigerator in a triangle formation, which allows for easy movement between these key areas.

Workflow: Keep frequently used items within arm's reach of where you'll be cooking. For example, store pots and pans near the stove and utensils near prep areas.

Step 3: Essential Storage Solutions

Efficient storage helps keep your kitchen organized and functional:

Cabinets and Drawers: Store cookware, dishes, and utensils in cabinets and drawers near their respective work areas. Use drawer dividers and organizers to keep utensils and tools neat.

Pantry Organization: Arrange pantry items logically with frequently used items at eye level and less used items higher or lower.

Hooks and Racks: Install hooks or racks on walls or inside cabinet doors to hang pots, pans, and utensils, freeing up cabinet space.

Step 4: Stock Your Kitchen with Essential Tools and Equipment

Ensure you have the necessary tools and equipment readily available:

Refer to the previous response on "Essential Tools and Equipment to Cook" for a comprehensive list.

Step 5: Create Efficient Prep Areas

Designate specific areas for meal preparation:

Countertops: Keep countertops clear of clutter to provide ample space for chopping, mixing, and assembling ingredients.

Cutting Boards: Place cutting boards near your prep area for easy access when chopping vegetables or preparing meat.

Step 6: Ensure Adequate Lighting and Ventilation

Good lighting and ventilation are crucial for a comfortable cooking environment:

Lighting: Install bright overhead lighting as well as task lighting under cabinets to illuminate workspaces.

Ventilation: If possible, have a range hood or extractor fan installed above your stove to remove cooking odors and steam.

Step 7: Personalize Your Kitchen with Comfortable Additions

Make your kitchen a pleasant place to cook:

Comfort Mats: Use anti-fatigue mats in areas where you stand for extended periods, such as in front of the sink or stove.

Decorative Touches: Add personal touches like plants, artwork, or decorative items to make your kitchen feel inviting.

Step 8: Maintain and Adapt as Needed

Regularly assess and adjust your kitchen setup to suit your evolving needs:

Maintenance: Keep your kitchen clean and organized to maintain an efficient workspace.

Adaptability: Be willing to rearrange items or add storage solutions as your cooking habits and needs change over time.

By following these steps, you can create a well-organized and functional kitchen space that makes cooking enjoyable and efficient. Tailor your setup to fit your cooking style and preferences, and don't hesitate to experiment with different arrangements until you find what works best for you.

Basic Kitchen Safety Tips

Practicing kitchen safety is crucial to prevent accidents and ensure a pleasant cooking experience. Here are some basic kitchen safety tips to follow when cooking:

Keep Your Workspace Clean and Clutter-Free:

Clear countertops of unnecessary items to have ample workspace.

Wipe up spills immediately to prevent slipping hazards.

Wash Your Hands Frequently:

Wash your hands thoroughly with soap and water before handling food, especially after handling raw meat, poultry, or fish.

Handle Knives and Sharp Objects Carefully:

Always use a sharp knife with a stable cutting surface (like a cutting board) to prevent slips.

Curl your fingers under and use a claw grip when chopping to avoid cutting yourself.

Use Heat Safely:

Turn pot handles inward on the stove to prevent accidental spills.

Use oven mitts or potholders to handle hot pans, pots, and dishes.

Keep flammable items such as dish towels, paper towels, and oven mitts away from open flames and hot surfaces.

Prevent Burns and Scalds:

Use long-handled utensils to stir food to avoid getting too close to heat sources.

Be cautious when opening hot oven doors and microwave lids to prevent steam burns.

Allow hot foods and liquids to cool slightly before tasting or pouring.

Monitor Cooking Closely:

Stay in the kitchen while cooking, especially when using the stove, oven, or deep fryer.

Use a timer to remind yourself when food is done to prevent burning or overcooking.

Handle Hot Oil with Care:

Use caution when frying food to avoid splattering hot oil.

If oil catches fire, turn off the heat and cover the pan with a metal lid or baking sheet to smother the flames. Never use water on a grease fire.

Be Aware of Food Safety:

Use separate cutting boards for raw meat, poultry, and seafood to avoid cross-contamination with other foods.

Cook food to the proper internal temperature using a food thermometer to ensure it's safe to eat.

Store Food Properly:

Refrigerate perishable foods promptly and store leftovers in airtight containers to prevent foodborne illnesses.

Maintain Smoke Alarms and Fire Extinguishers:

Ensure smoke alarms are working and have fire extinguishers on hand in case of emergencies.

By following these basic kitchen safety tips, you can create a safe environment for cooking and reduce the risk of accidents or injuries. Developing good habits and being aware of potential hazards will help you enjoy your time in the kitchen while keeping yourself and others safe.

Understanding Cooking Terms and Techniques

Understanding cooking terms and techniques is fundamental for becoming a proficient cook. Here's a comprehensive guide to common cooking terms and techniques:

Cooking Terms:

Bake: To cook food using dry heat in an oven.

Boil: To heat a liquid until bubbles break continuously on the surface.

Braise: To cook food slowly in a small amount of liquid in a covered pot.

Broil: To cook food under direct heat in an oven or grill.

Caramelize: To heat sugar until it melts and turns brown.

Deglaze: To add liquid to a hot pan to dissolve cooked-on bits of food for making sauces.

Dice: To cut food into small cubes.

Grate: To shred food into fine pieces using a grater.

Julienne: To cut food into thin matchstick-shaped pieces.

Knead: To work dough with hands to develop gluten.

Mince: To chop food into very fine pieces.

Poach: To cook food gently in liquid just below boiling point.

Roast: To cook food uncovered in an oven, often with dry heat.

Sauté: To cook food quickly in a small amount of oil or butter over high heat.

Simmer: To cook food gently in liquid over low heat.

Steam: To cook food over boiling water in a covered pot or steamer basket.

Whisk: To beat ingredients quickly with a whisk to incorporate air.

Cooking Techniques:

Grilling: Cooking food directly over an open flame or heat source.

Frying: Cooking food in hot oil or fat.

Steaming: Cooking food by surrounding it with steam in a covered pot or steamer.

Baking: Cooking food using dry heat in an oven, typically for bread, cakes, and pastries.

Broiling: Cooking food by exposing it to direct heat from above.

Sauteing: Cooking food quickly in a small amount of oil or butter over high heat.

Braising: Cooking food slowly in a covered pot with a small amount of liquid.

Roasting: Cooking food uncovered in an oven with dry heat, often for meats and vegetables.

Poaching: Cooking food gently in liquid just below boiling point.

Blanching: Briefly cooking food in boiling water, then plunging it into ice water to stop cooking.

Deglazing: Adding liquid to a hot pan to dissolve cooked-on bits of food and make a sauce.

Marinating: Soaking food in a mixture of ingredients to add flavor before cooking.

Flambéing: Igniting alcohol in a hot pan to create a burst of flames.

Sous Vide: Cooking food in vacuum-sealed bags in a water bath at precise temperatures.

Dredging: Coating food with flour or breadcrumbs before cooking.

Understanding these terms and techniques will help you follow recipes accurately, experiment with different cooking methods, and ultimately become more confident and versatile in the kitchen. Practice and familiarity with these concepts will enhance your cooking skills and allow you to create delicious meals with ease.

Knife Skills: Chopping, Dicing, and Slicing

Knife skills are essential for efficient and safe cooking. Mastering chopping, dicing, and slicing techniques will not only improve your cooking speed but also ensure consistent and professional-looking results. Here's a guide to each technique:

1. Chopping:

Purpose: To cut food into irregular pieces, typically larger than diced pieces.

Technique:

✓ Start with a sharp chef's knife and a stable cutting board.

✓ Hold the food with your non-dominant hand, keeping fingers curled under for safety.

✓ With a rocking motion, bring the knife down through the food using the full length of the blade.

✓ Maintain a steady rhythm to achieve evenly chopped pieces.

✓ Rotate the food as needed to maintain control and continue chopping until pieces are of desired size.

Examples: Chopping onions, bell peppers, herbs, or nuts for salads or garnishes.

2. Dicing:

Purpose: To cut food into small, uniform cubes.

Technique:

✓ Begin with a peeled and trimmed piece of food on the cutting board.

✓ Slice the food crosswise into planks of even thickness.

✓ Stack the planks and cut them into sticks of desired width.

✓ Finally, cut across the sticks to create small cubes.

Examples: Dicing vegetables like carrots, potatoes, or tomatoes for soups, stews, or sauces.

3. Slicing:

Purpose: To cut food into thin, uniform pieces.

Technique:

✓ Position the food securely on the cutting board.

✓ Hold the food steady with your non-dominant hand, using a claw grip to protect your fingers.

✓ Slice through the food using a smooth, controlled motion with the knife blade.

✓ Maintain consistent thickness by guiding the knife evenly through the food.

Examples: Slicing meats, fruits, or vegetables for stir-fries, sandwiches, or garnishes.

Tips for Knife Skills:

Use a Sharp Knife: A sharp knife is safer and more efficient than a dull one. Sharpen your knives regularly to maintain their edge.

Practice Safety: Always curl your fingers under and use a claw grip when holding food. Keep the knife blade in contact with the cutting board to prevent accidents.

Maintain Control: Use a stable cutting board and a non-slip surface to ensure stability while cutting.

Consistency: Aim for consistent size and shape to ensure even cooking and attractive presentation.

Practice Patience: Developing knife skills takes practice. Start with slow, deliberate movements, and gradually increase speed as you become more confident.

By mastering these basic knife skills—chopping, dicing, and slicing—you'll not only enhance your cooking efficiency but also elevate the quality and presentation of your dishes. Remember, practice and patience are key to becoming proficient in any culinary technique.

Cooking Methods: Sauteing, Boiling, Roasting, and Grilling

Understanding different cooking methods allows you to prepare a wide variety of dishes with different flavors and textures. Here's a guide to four common cooking methods: sautéing, boiling, roasting, and grilling.

1. Sautéing:

Purpose: To cook food quickly over medium to high heat in a small amount of oil or fat.

Technique:

1. Heat a sauté pan or skillet over medium-high heat.
2. Add a small amount of oil or butter to coat the bottom of the pan.
3. Once hot, add the food (usually small pieces) in a single layer.
4. Use a spatula or tongs to move the food around constantly to ensure even cooking and prevent burning.
5. Cook until food is browned and cooked through, typically a few minutes depending on the size and type of food.

Examples: Sautéing is great for cooking vegetables, meats, seafood, and tofu quickly while preserving their natural flavors and textures.

2. Boiling:

Purpose: To cook food in boiling water or liquid.

Technique:

1. Bring a pot of water or broth to a rolling boil over high heat.
2. Add salt if desired (helps flavor the food).
3. Carefully add the food (such as pasta, vegetables, or eggs).
4. Cook until food is tender or reaches desired doneness, stirring occasionally.
5. Drain food using a colander or slotted spoon.

Examples: Boiling is commonly used for pasta, rice, potatoes, vegetables, eggs, and grains.

3. Roasting:

Purpose: To cook food, usually meat or vegetables, uncovered in an oven using dry heat.

Technique:

1. Preheat your oven to the desired temperature (often between 350°F to 450°F depending on the recipe).
2. Arrange food on a baking sheet or roasting pan in a single layer.
3. Drizzle with oil, season with salt, pepper, and any desired herbs or spices.
4. Place in the oven and roast until food is browned and cooked through, turning occasionally for even cooking.

Examples: Roasting is excellent for meats (like chicken, beef, or pork) and vegetables (such as potatoes, carrots, or Brussels sprouts) to enhance their flavors through caramelization.

4. Grilling:

Purpose: To cook food over direct heat from below, typically outdoors on a grill or indoors on a grill pan.

Technique:

1. Preheat your grill or grill pan to medium-high heat.
2. Lightly oil the grill grates or grill pan to prevent sticking.
3. Place food on the grill and cook, turning occasionally, until grill marks form and food is cooked to desired doneness.

Examples: Grilling is perfect for cooking meats (like steak, burgers, or chicken breasts), seafood (such as shrimp or salmon), vegetables (like asparagus or bell peppers), and even fruits (like pineapple or peaches).

Tips for Cooking Methods:

Temperature Control: Mastering temperature control is crucial for each method to achieve the desired results—whether it's searing for sautéing, maintaining a rolling boil for boiling, adjusting oven temperature for roasting, or managing grill heat for grilling.

Flavor Enhancement: Each method offers unique opportunities to enhance flavors through techniques like searing, caramelization (in roasting), and imparting smoky flavors (in grilling).

Adaptability: Many recipes combine these methods (e.g., sautéing vegetables before roasting or finishing meats with a grill for charred flavor).

By understanding and practicing these cooking methods—sauteing, boiling, roasting, and grilling—you'll have the foundation to create a wide range of delicious and satisfying dishes tailored to your preferences and culinary aspirations.

Understanding Heat Control

Understanding heat control is essential for successful cooking, as it allows you to achieve the desired results in terms of texture, flavor, and appearance. Here's a comprehensive guide to understanding heat control in cooking:

Types of Heat:

Direct Heat:

> **Sautéing and Stir-frying**: Cooking food quickly over high heat in a pan with a small amount of oil or butter.

> **Grilling**: Cooking food directly over an open flame or heat source, typically outdoors on a grill or indoors on a grill pan.

Indirect Heat:

> **Baking and Roasting**: Cooking food in an oven using surrounding dry heat.

> **Simmering and Boiling**: Cooking food in a liquid at a temperature just below boiling point.

Factors Affecting Heat Control:

Heat Source:

> Gas vs. Electric: Gas stoves provide instant and responsive heat control, while electric stoves may have a slight delay in temperature adjustment.

> Oven Types: Conventional ovens provide even heat distribution, while convection ovens use fans to circulate hot air for faster cooking.

Temperature Settings:

> Stovetops: Use knobs or dials to adjust heat levels from low to high.

> Ovens: Set temperatures ranging from low (around 200°F) to high (up to 500°F or more), depending on the recipe requirements.

Cookware and Utensils:

Heat Conductivity: Choose pots and pans with good heat conductivity to ensure even cooking.

Utensils: Use heat-resistant utensils for stirring and turning food to avoid melting or damage.

Techniques for Heat Control:

Preheating:

Preheat pans and ovens before cooking to ensure even heat distribution and consistent cooking.

Adjusting Heat Levels:

Use high heat for searing and browning (e.g., sautéing meats).

Medium heat for cooking vegetables and simmering sauces.

Low heat for gentle cooking, melting, or keeping food warm.

Managing Cooking Times:

Follow recipe instructions for cooking times based on heat settings and desired doneness.

Monitor food closely, adjusting heat as needed to prevent burning or undercooking.

Resting and Carryover Cooking:

Allow food to rest after cooking to finish cooking through residual heat (carryover cooking).

This is especially important for meats to redistribute juices and ensure tenderness.

Tips for Effective Heat Control:

Use a Thermometer: Use a meat thermometer to check internal temperatures for meats to ensure they are cooked to safe levels without overcooking.

Practice Patience: Avoid raising heat levels too quickly; allow time for pans and ovens to reach desired temperatures gradually.

Experiment and Learn: Get familiar with your equipment and how it responds to different heat settings and cooking techniques through practice.

Understanding heat control not only helps you achieve better cooking results but also enhances your confidence and ability to improvise in the kitchen. With practice and attention to detail, you'll develop the skills needed to master the art of cooking with precision and creativity.

Understanding Herbs, Spices, and Seasonings

Understanding herbs, spices, and seasonings is essential for adding depth, flavor, and complexity to your cooking. Here's a comprehensive guide to each category:

Herbs:

Herbs are the leaves of plants used for flavoring, typically harvested fresh or dried.

Common Herbs and Their Uses:

Basil: Fresh and aromatic, used in Italian dishes, pesto, salads, and soups.

Parsley: Fresh and mild, used as a garnish, in sauces, salads, and soups.

Thyme: Earthy and versatile, used in roasts, stews, soups, and marinades.

Rosemary: Woody and aromatic, used with roasted meats, potatoes, and bread.

Cilantro (Coriander): Fresh and citrusy, used in Mexican, Indian, and Southeast Asian cuisines.

Mint: Refreshing and cooling, used in desserts, drinks, salads, and sauces.

How to Use:

Fresh Herbs: Add near the end of cooking or as a garnish for maximum flavor.

Dried Herbs: Use in cooking processes early on to allow flavors to meld.

Spices:

Spices are dried seeds, fruits, roots, or bark of plants used to add flavor and aroma to dishes.

Common Spices and Their Uses:

Cinnamon: Warm and sweet, used in baking, desserts, curries, and beverages.

Cumin: Earthy and nutty, used in Indian, Mexican, and Middle Eastern cuisines.

Paprika: Mild and slightly sweet, used in rubs, stews, soups, and as a garnish.

Turmeric: Earthy and slightly bitter, used in curries, rice dishes, and as a natural coloring agent.

Chili Powder: Spicy and smoky, used in Tex-Mex dishes, chili, and marinades.

Ginger: Warm and pungent, used in Asian stir-fries, marinades, and desserts.

How to Use:

Whole Spices: Toast before grinding for enhanced flavor, or use in simmered dishes.

Ground Spices: Add during cooking to release flavors evenly throughout the dish.

Seasonings:

Seasonings include salts, blends, and other flavor enhancers used to season food.

Common Seasonings:

Salt: Enhances natural flavors and balances sweetness and acidity in dishes.

Black Pepper: Adds heat and depth to savory dishes, sauces, and marinades.

Garlic Powder: Provides a savory and aromatic flavor, used in various cuisines.

Onion Powder: Adds sweetness and depth, used in soups, stews, and sauces.

Italian Seasoning: Blend of herbs like oregano, basil, and thyme, used in Italian-inspired dishes.

Cajun Seasoning: Spicy and savory blend, used in Cajun and Creole cooking.

How to Use:

Use sparingly to enhance flavors without overpowering the dish.

Experiment with different blends and combinations to suit your taste preferences.

Tips for Using Herbs, Spices, and Seasonings:

◇ **Balance**: Aim for a balance of flavors—sweet, salty, sour, bitter, and umami—to create well-rounded dishes.

◇ **Fresh vs. Dried**: Use fresh herbs for bright flavors and dried herbs for concentrated flavors.

◇ **Experiment**: Don't be afraid to experiment with different herbs, spices, and seasonings to discover new flavor profiles and enhance your cooking skills.

By understanding and mastering the use of herbs, spices, and seasonings, you can elevate your dishes from ordinary to extraordinary, adding depth and complexity that will delight your taste buds and impress your guests.

Balancing Flavors: Sweet, Sour, Salty, Bitter, Umami

Balancing flavors—sweet, sour, salty, bitter, and umami—is key to creating delicious and well-rounded dishes. Here's a guide on each flavor component and how to achieve balance in your cooking:

1. Sweet:

Flavor Profile: Sweetness adds a pleasant, sugary taste to dishes.

Examples: Sugar, honey, fruits (like mango or berries), caramelized onions.

Balancing Tip: Use sweetness to complement savory or spicy dishes, but avoid overpowering other flavors.

2. Sour:

Flavor Profile: Sourness provides acidity and tanginess.

Examples: Citrus fruits (like lemon or lime), vinegar, yogurt, sour cream.

Balancing Tip: Use sourness to brighten flavors and add freshness; balance with sweetness or saltiness.

3. Salty:

Flavor Profile: Saltiness enhances and balances other flavors.

Examples: Salt, soy sauce, cured meats (like bacon), olives.

Balancing Tip: Use salt to heighten flavors and create contrast; be mindful of not oversalting.

4. Bitter:

Flavor Profile: Bitterness adds a complex, slightly sharp taste.

Examples: Dark leafy greens (like kale), coffee, dark chocolate, some herbs (like arugula or dandelion greens).

Balancing Tip: Balance bitterness with sweetness or acidity; use in moderation to add depth without overwhelming.

5. Umami:

Flavor Profile: Umami provides a savory, meaty taste.

Examples: Soy sauce, mushrooms, tomatoes, Parmesan cheese, miso paste.

Balancing Tip: Enhance savory dishes with umami-rich ingredients; balance with other flavors for complexity.

Tips for Balancing Flavors:

Taste as You Cook: Regularly taste your food and adjust flavors as needed to achieve balance.

Layer Flavors: Build flavors gradually by adding ingredients at different stages of cooking.

Contrast and Complement: Aim for a harmonious blend of flavors that both contrast and complement each other.

Example of Flavor Balancing in Cooking:

Stir-Fry: Start with a base of soy sauce (salty), add a squeeze of lime juice (sour), a touch of honey (sweet), and finish with umami-rich ingredients like mushrooms or oyster sauce. Garnish with fresh herbs or toasted sesame seeds for added complexity.

Salad Dressing: Combine olive oil (rich and slightly bitter), balsamic vinegar (sour), a pinch of salt (salty), a touch of honey (sweet), and finish with grated Parmesan cheese (umami) to balance flavors in a salad.

By understanding and mastering the balance of sweet, sour, salty, bitter, and umami flavors, you can create dishes that are not only delicious but also nuanced and satisfying. Experiment with different ingredients and proportions to discover your preferred flavor profiles and enhance your culinary skills.

Creating Homemade Stocks and Sauces

Creating homemade stocks and sauces is a wonderful way to elevate your cooking with rich flavors and depth. Here's a guide to making both:

Homemade Stocks

Stocks form the foundation of many dishes, providing a flavorful liquid base for soups, stews, sauces, and risottos.

Ingredients for a Basic Stock:

Chicken Stock:

1. Chicken bones (such as carcasses or wings)

2. Water

3. Onion, carrots, celery (optional, for flavor)

4. Garlic, parsley, thyme, bay leaves (optional, for aromatics)

5. Salt and pepper to taste

Vegetable Stock:

1. Assorted vegetables (such as onions, carrots, celery, mushrooms, leeks)

2. Water

3. Garlic, parsley, thyme, bay leaves (optional, for aromatics)

4. Salt and pepper to taste

Method

Preparation:

1. For meat-based stocks, roast bones in the oven until browned for richer flavor.

2. Wash and roughly chop vegetables.

Cooking:

1. Place bones or vegetables in a large pot and cover with water (usually 2-3 times the volume of bones or vegetables).

2. Bring to a boil, then reduce heat to a simmer.

3. Skim off any foam that rises to the surface.

4. Add aromatics and seasonings.

5. Simmer gently for 2-4 hours (longer for meat stocks) to extract flavors.

Straining:

1. Remove from heat and strain through a fine mesh sieve or cheesecloth.

2. Discard solids.

Storage:

1. Use immediately in recipes or cool completely before storing in containers.

2. Refrigerate for up to 3-4 days or freeze for longer storage.

Homemade Sauces:

Sauces add flavor, moisture, and texture to dishes, enhancing their overall appeal.

Ingredients for Basic Sauces:

Tomato Sauce:

1. Tomatoes (fresh or canned)

2. Olive oil

3. Onion, garlic

4. Herbs (like basil, oregano)

5. Salt and pepper to taste

Bechamel Sauce (White Sauce):

1. Butter

2. Flour

3. Milk

4. Nutmeg, salt, and pepper to taste

Hollandaise Sauce:

1. Egg yolks

2. Butter

3. Lemon juice or vinegar

4. Salt and cayenne pepper to taste

Method

Preparation:

1. For tomato sauce, sauté onions and garlic in olive oil until soft, then add tomatoes and herbs, simmer until thickened.

2. For bechamel, melt butter in a saucepan, stir in flour to make a roux, gradually whisk in milk until thickened.

3. For hollandaise, whisk egg yolks and lemon juice in a bowl over simmering water, gradually whisk in melted butter until thickened.

Cooking

1. Cook sauces over low to medium heat, stirring constantly to prevent sticking or burning.

Adjusting Consistency and Seasoning

1. Add more liquid to thin sauces or simmer longer to thicken.

2. Season with salt, pepper, and other herbs/spices to taste.

Storage

1. Use immediately or cool completely before storing in airtight containers.

2. Refrigerate for a few days or freeze for longer storage.

Tips for Success:

✓ **Quality Ingredients**: Use fresh, high-quality ingredients for the best flavor.

✓ **Patience**: Allow stocks and sauces to simmer gently to develop flavors.

✓ **Experiment**: Customize flavors with different herbs, spices, and seasonings to suit your taste preferences.

✓ **Batch Cooking**: Make larger quantities and freeze in portions for convenient use.

Creating homemade stocks and sauces not only enhances the taste of your dishes but also allows you to control ingredients and customize flavors to your liking. With practice and creativity, you'll master these techniques and elevate your culinary skills significantly.

Chapter 5: Exploring Ingredients

Choosing Fresh Produce

Choosing fresh produce is essential for ensuring your dishes taste their best and are packed with nutrients. Here are some tips for selecting the freshest fruits and vegetables:

General Tips for Fresh Produce

Appearance:

Look for produce that is vibrant in color, free from bruises, blemishes, or mold.

Avoid fruits and vegetables that are overly soft, wrinkled, or have spots of discoloration.

Texture:

Choose fruits that feel firm and heavy for their size (e.g., apples, citrus fruits).

Vegetables should be crisp and firm (e.g., carrots, bell peppers).

Smell:

Some fruits and vegetables have a characteristic aroma when ripe (e.g., melons, berries).

Avoid produce with an unpleasant or moldy smell.

Seasonality:

Buy produce that is in season for the best flavor and nutritional value.

Check local farmers' markets or consult seasonal produce guides.

Tips for Specific Types of Produce

Fruits

Citrus Fruits (e.g., oranges, lemons):

Choose fruits that feel heavy for their size and have smooth, brightly colored skins.

Avoid fruits with soft spots or a dull appearance.

Berries (e.g., strawberries, blueberries):

Look for plump, brightly colored berries with fresh green caps (for strawberries).

Avoid berries that are mushy, moldy, or have a dull appearance.

Apples

Select apples that are firm and have smooth, unblemished skin.

Avoid apples with wrinkles, soft spots, or bruises.

Vegetables

Leafy Greens (e.g., spinach, kale):

Choose greens with crisp leaves and vibrant colors.

Avoid wilted, yellowed, or slimy leaves.

Root Vegetables (e.g., carrots, potatoes):

Select vegetables that are firm with smooth skins and no sprouting.

Avoid soft spots, wrinkles, or green patches on potatoes.

Tomatoes

Choose tomatoes that are firm yet slightly yielding to gentle pressure.

Look for tomatoes with smooth, shiny skins and bright color.

Avoid tomatoes that are too soft, wrinkled, or have bruises.

Storage Tips

✓ **Refrigerate** fruits and vegetables that are prone to spoilage, such as berries, leafy greens, and cut fruits.

✓ **Store** root vegetables, potatoes, and tomatoes in a cool, dry place away from direct sunlight.

✓ **Use** herbs promptly or store them wrapped in a damp paper towel in a plastic bag in the refrigerator to maintain freshness.

By following these tips, you'll be able to choose fresh produce that enhances your cooking, providing optimal flavor, texture, and nutrition for your dishes. Experiment with different varieties and seasonal options to discover new flavors and enjoy the benefits of fresh, wholesome ingredients in your meals.

Selecting Quality Meats and Poultry

Selecting quality meats and poultry is crucial for ensuring delicious and safe meals. Here are some tips to help you choose the best options:

General Tips for Selecting Meats and Poultry

Appearance:

✓ Look for meats that are bright and vibrant in color. Beef should be bright red, while pork should be pinkish-red. Poultry should have a pinkish or whitish color.

✓ Avoid meats that are dull, grayish, or have any discoloration.

Texture:

✓ Meat should feel firm to the touch. Press gently; it should bounce back slightly and not leave an indentation.

✓ Poultry skin should be smooth and unbroken.

Marbling:

✓ For beef, look for marbling (white flecks of fat within the muscle). Marbling enhances tenderness and flavor.

✓ Pork and poultry should have a moderate amount of fat for juiciness but not excessive amounts.

Odor:

✓ Fresh meats should have a neutral odor or a slightly metallic smell.

✓ Avoid meats with a sour, ammonia-like, or strong odor, as these can indicate spoilage.

Packaging:

Choose meats and poultry that are well-sealed and cold to the touch when purchasing from a butcher or supermarket.

Tips for Specific Types of Meat and Poultry:

Beef

Cuts:

✓ Choose cuts that are bright red with marbling for tenderness and flavor.

✓ Prime cuts (e.g., ribeye, tenderloin) are typically more tender and flavorful than lean cuts (e.g., round, sirloin).

Grades:

✓ USDA grading (Prime, Choice, Select) can indicate quality and tenderness. Prime is the highest grade, followed by Choice and Select.

Pork

Color and Texture:

✓ Pork should be pinkish-red in color, with a moderate amount of fat for juiciness.

✓ Look for cuts with a smooth texture and no excessive fat or gristle.

Freshness:

✓ Choose pork that is freshly butchered and has a clean, fresh odor.

Poultry

Skin and Appearance:

✓ Poultry skin should be smooth, unbroken, and free of blemishes.

✓ The flesh should be plump and moist, without any discoloration or strong odor.

Packaging and Labels:

✓ Look for poultry that is labeled with information on its origin, such as organic, free-range, or pasture-raised options.

✓ Check for the absence of added hormones or antibiotics if that is a concern for you.

Storage and Handling:

Refrigerate meats and poultry promptly after purchase, and use or freeze within a few days to maintain freshness.

Thaw frozen meats and poultry in the refrigerator or under cold running water, not at room temperature, to prevent bacterial growth.

Cook meats and poultry to the appropriate internal temperature to ensure safety (e.g., 145°F for beef, 165°F for poultry).

By following these tips, you'll be able to select high-quality meats and poultry that are not only safe to eat but also enhance the flavor and enjoyment of your meals. Whether you're grilling, roasting, or sautéing, starting with quality ingredients is key to creating delicious dishes for yourself and your loved ones.

Using Dairy and Non-Dairy Substitutes

Using dairy and non-dairy substitutes can accommodate dietary preferences, allergies, or health considerations without sacrificing flavor or texture in your recipes. Here's a guide on how to effectively use both:

Dairy Substitutes

Milk:

Substitutes: Almond milk, soy milk, oat milk, coconut milk, rice milk.

Usage: Use these substitutes in equal amounts as regular milk in recipes for baking, cooking, or beverages.

Butter

Substitutes: Margarine, vegan butter (made from oils like coconut, soy, or palm), coconut oil (in some baking recipes).

Usage: Substitute equal amounts in recipes for baking, cooking, or spreading.

Yogurt

Substitutes: Dairy-free yogurt (almond, coconut, soy, oat), Greek yogurt alternatives.

Usage: Use in recipes for marinades, dressings, smoothies, or as a topping.

Cheese

Substitutes: Plant-based cheeses (made from nuts like cashews, almonds, or soy), nutritional yeast (for a cheesy flavor), vegan cheese alternatives.

Usage: Use in recipes for melting, grating, or spreading on sandwiches or crackers.

Tips for Using Dairy Substitutes

Texture and Consistency: Dairy substitutes may have different textures and consistencies than their dairy counterparts. Experiment to find the best match for your recipe.

Flavor Adjustments: Some substitutes may impart different flavors. Adjust seasonings or ingredients as needed to balance flavors.

Baking: When baking with dairy substitutes, consider that the fat content and moisture level may affect the texture and rise of baked goods. Adjust other ingredients as necessary.

Non-Dairy Substitutes

Nut Milk (Almond, Cashew, etc.)

Usage: Use in place of dairy milk in cereals, smoothies, coffee, and baking recipes.

Coconut Milk

Usage: Ideal for soups, curries, sauces, desserts, and beverages.

Soy Milk

Usage: Suitable for baking, cooking, and beverages due to its neutral flavor and creamy texture.

Oat Milk

Usage: Great for coffee, lattes, smoothies, cereals, and baking.

Benefits of Non-Dairy Substitutes

Allergen-Friendly: Ideal for those with dairy allergies or lactose intolerance.

Health Considerations: Lower in cholesterol and saturated fats compared to dairy products.

Environmental Impact: Often more sustainable and eco-friendlier than traditional dairy products.

Cooking Tips

Heat Stability: Some non-dairy substitutes may curdle or separate when heated. Choose options that are labeled as suitable for cooking and baking.

Thickening Agents: Non-dairy substitutes may require thickening agents (like cornstarch or arrowroot) in recipes that call for dairy cream or milk.

Flavor Profile: Experiment with different non-dairy options to find the ones that best complement your recipes in terms of taste and texture.

By incorporating both dairy and non-dairy substitutes into your cooking and baking, you can cater to various dietary needs and preferences while still enjoying delicious and flavorful dishes. Whether you're making creamy sauces, baking desserts, or simply enjoying a beverage, there are versatile substitutes available to suit your culinary needs.

Breakfast Favorites: Pancakes, Omelets, and Smoothies

Breakfast is a delightful meal that can be both comforting and nutritious. Here's how to prepare some popular breakfast favorites: pancakes, omelets, and smoothies.

Pancakes

Ingredients:

1 cup all-purpose flour

1 tablespoon sugar

1 teaspoon baking powder

1/2 teaspoon baking soda

1/4 teaspoon salt

1 cup milk (dairy or non-dairy)

1 large egg

2 tablespoons melted butter or oil

Optional: vanilla extract, cinnamon, blueberries, chocolate chips

Instructions:

1. In a large bowl, whisk together the flour, sugar, baking powder, baking soda, and salt.

2. In another bowl, whisk together the milk, egg, melted butter or oil, and any optional ingredients.

3. Pour the wet ingredients into the dry ingredients and stir until just combined. It's okay if the batter is slightly lumpy.

4. Heat a non-stick skillet or griddle over medium heat. Lightly grease with butter or oil.

5. Pour 1/4 cup of batter onto the skillet for each pancake. Cook until bubbles form on the surface and the edges look set, about 2-3 minutes.

6. Flip the pancakes and cook until golden brown on the other side, about 1-2 minutes more.

7. Serve warm with maple syrup, fresh fruit, whipped cream, or your favorite toppings.

Omelets

Ingredients:

2 large eggs

2 tablespoons milk or water

Salt and pepper, to taste

Fillings: diced vegetables (bell peppers, onions, tomatoes), cooked meats (ham, bacon), cheese (cheddar, feta), herbs (parsley, chives)

Instructions:

1. Crack the eggs into a bowl, add milk or water, and whisk until well combined. Season with salt and pepper.

2. Heat a non-stick skillet over medium heat. Add a small amount of butter or oil.

3. Pour the egg mixture into the skillet. As the eggs start to set around the edges, use a spatula to gently push the cooked eggs toward the center, tilting the skillet to let the uncooked eggs flow to the edges.

4. Continue cooking until the eggs are mostly set but still slightly runny on top.

5. Add your desired fillings to one half of the omelet.

6. Fold the omelet in half with a spatula and cook for another minute until the cheese melts and the filling is heated through.

7. Slide the omelet onto a plate and serve immediately.

Smoothies

Ingredients:

1 cup frozen fruit (berries, mango, pineapple)

1 ripe banana

1 cup milk or dairy-free alternative (almond milk, soy milk, coconut water)

1/2 cup yogurt (Greek yogurt, coconut yogurt)

Optional: honey or maple syrup, protein powder, spinach or kale (for green smoothies)

Instructions:

1. Place all ingredients in a blender.

2. Blend until smooth and creamy, adding more liquid as needed to reach your desired consistency.

3. Taste and adjust sweetness, if necessary, with honey or maple syrup.

4. Pour into glasses and serve immediately.

Tips

Variations: Experiment with different pancake toppings (fruits, nuts, chocolate) or omelet fillings (spinach, mushrooms).

Nutritional Boost: Add chia seeds, flaxseeds, or protein powder to smoothies for extra nutrition.

Make Ahead: Pancake batter can be prepared ahead and stored in the fridge overnight. Smoothie ingredients can be prepped the night before for a quick blend in the morning.

Enjoy these breakfast favorites as a delicious start to your day, whether you prefer a hearty omelet, fluffy pancakes, or a refreshing smoothie packed with nutrients.

Lunchtime Classics: Salads, Sandwiches, and Soups

Lunchtime offers a variety of classics that are not only delicious but also satisfying and easy to prepare. Here's how to make some popular lunchtime favorites: salads, sandwiches, and soups.

Salads

Classic Garden Salad:

Ingredients:

Mixed greens (lettuce, spinach, arugula)

Cherry tomatoes, halved

Cucumber, sliced

Red onion, thinly sliced

Carrots, shredded

Bell peppers, sliced

Optional: avocado, olives, croutons, feta cheese

Instructions:

1. Wash and prepare all vegetables as needed.

2. In a large bowl, toss together the mixed greens, cherry tomatoes, cucumber, red onion, carrots, and bell peppers.

3. Add any optional ingredients as desired.

4. Drizzle with your favorite salad dressing (such as balsamic vinaigrette, ranch, or lemon vinaigrette) and toss to coat.

5. Serve immediately as a refreshing and nutritious lunch option.

Sandwiches

Classic Turkey and Avocado Sandwich:

Ingredients:

Sliced whole grain bread

Sliced turkey breast

Avocado, sliced

Tomato, sliced

Lettuce leaves

Mustard or mayonnaise

Optional: cheese (cheddar, Swiss), pickles, sprouts

Instructions:

1. Toast the bread slices lightly, if desired.

2. Spread mustard or mayonnaise on one side of each bread slice.

3. Layer one slice of bread with turkey slices, avocado slices, tomato slices, lettuce leaves, and any optional ingredients.

4. Top with the second slice of bread, mustard or mayonnaise side down.

5. Cut the sandwich in half diagonally or vertically and serve immediately.

Soups

Classic Tomato Soup:

Ingredients:

2 tablespoons olive oil

1 onion, chopped

2 cloves garlic, minced

2 cans (14 oz each) diced tomatoes

1 cup vegetable or chicken broth

1 teaspoon dried basil

Salt and pepper, to taste

1/2 cup heavy cream or coconut milk (for a dairy-free option)

Fresh basil leaves, for garnish

Instructions:

1. Heat olive oil in a large pot over medium heat.

2. Add chopped onion and cook until translucent, about 5-7 minutes.

3. Add minced garlic and cook for another minute until fragrant.

4. Stir in diced tomatoes (with their juices), vegetable or chicken broth, dried basil, salt, and pepper.

5. Bring to a boil, then reduce heat and simmer for 15-20 minutes, stirring occasionally.

6. Use an immersion blender to puree the soup until smooth. Alternatively, transfer to a blender in batches and blend until smooth, then return to the pot.

7. Stir in heavy cream or coconut milk and heat through.

8. Taste and adjust seasoning if needed.

9. Ladle into bowls, garnish with fresh basil leaves, and serve hot with a side of crusty bread or a grilled cheese sandwich.

Tips

◇ **Preparation**: Prep ingredients ahead of time to assemble quickly during lunchtime.

◇ **Variations**: Customize salads, sandwiches, and soups with your favorite ingredients and flavors.

◇ **Make Ahead**: Soups and salads can often be made ahead and stored in the refrigerator for a few days, allowing flavors to meld.

Enjoy these lunchtime classics as delicious and satisfying options that can be easily customized to suit your taste preferences and dietary needs. Whether you're enjoying a hearty salad, a comforting sandwich, or a warm bowl of soup, these meals are sure to brighten your lunch break.

Dinner Delights: Pasta, Stir-fries, and Casseroles

Dinner delights come in various forms, from comforting pasta dishes to flavorful stir-fries and hearty casseroles. Here's how to prepare each of these dinner classics:

Pasta

Classic Spaghetti Carbonara:

Ingredients:

8 oz spaghetti or linguine

4 oz pancetta or bacon, diced

2 cloves garlic, minced

2 large eggs

1/2 cup grated Parmesan cheese, plus extra for serving

Salt and black pepper, to taste

Fresh parsley, chopped (optional)

Instructions:

1. Cook pasta in a large pot of salted boiling water according to package instructions until al dente. Reserve 1 cup of pasta water, then drain the pasta.

2. While pasta is cooking, heat a large skillet over medium heat. Add diced pancetta or bacon and cook until crispy, about 5-7 minutes.

3. Add minced garlic to the skillet and cook for 1 minute until fragrant.

4. In a bowl, whisk together eggs, grated Parmesan cheese, and a pinch of black pepper.

5. Remove skillet from heat. Quickly toss the hot drained pasta with the pancetta and garlic mixture.

6. Pour the egg mixture over the hot pasta, stirring quickly to coat the pasta evenly. The heat from the pasta will cook the eggs into a creamy sauce. If needed, add reserved pasta water a little at a time to adjust consistency.

7. Season with salt and more black pepper to taste. Garnish with chopped fresh parsley and additional grated Parmesan cheese.

8. Serve immediately, ensuring each portion is creamy and well-coated with the sauce.

Stir-fries

Chicken and Vegetable Stir-fry:

Ingredients:

1 lb boneless, skinless chicken breasts, thinly sliced

2 tablespoons soy sauce

1 tablespoon oyster sauce

1 tablespoon cornstarch

2 tablespoons vegetable oil, divided

1 onion, thinly sliced

2 bell peppers (any color), thinly sliced

1 cup broccoli florets

2 cloves garlic, minced

1 teaspoon grated ginger

Cooked rice or noodles, for serving

Instructions:

1. In a bowl, combine sliced chicken with soy sauce, oyster sauce, and cornstarch. Mix well and set aside to marinate for 10-15 minutes.

2. Heat 1 tablespoon of vegetable oil in a large skillet or wok over medium-high heat.

3. Add marinated chicken and stir-fry until cooked through and lightly browned, about 5-7 minutes. Remove chicken from skillet and set aside.

4. Heat remaining tablespoon of vegetable oil in the same skillet.

5. Add sliced onion, bell peppers, and broccoli florets. Stir-fry for 3-4 minutes until vegetables are tender-crisp.

6. Add minced garlic and grated ginger to the skillet. Stir-fry for another minute until fragrant.

7. Return cooked chicken to the skillet and toss everything together until well combined and heated through.

8. Serve hot stir-fry over cooked rice or noodles.

Casseroles

Classic Beef and Potato Casserole:

Ingredients:

1 lb ground beef

1 onion, chopped

2 cloves garlic, minced

1 can (10.75 oz) condensed cream of mushroom soup

1/2 cup milk

2 cups frozen mixed vegetables (carrots, peas, corn)

4 cups cooked potatoes, diced (about 4 medium potatoes)

1 cup shredded cheddar cheese

Salt and black pepper, to taste

Fresh parsley, chopped (optional)

Instructions:

1. Preheat oven to 350°F (175°C). Grease a 9x13-inch baking dish.

2. In a large skillet, cook ground beef over medium heat until browned. Drain excess fat.

3. Add chopped onion and minced garlic to the skillet. Cook for 3-4 minutes until onion is softened.

4. Stir in condensed cream of mushroom soup and milk. Mix well until combined.

5. Add frozen mixed vegetables and cooked diced potatoes to the skillet. Stir to combine everything evenly.

6. Season with salt and black pepper to taste.

7. Transfer mixture to the prepared baking dish. Spread evenly and sprinkle shredded cheddar cheese over the top.

8. Cover with foil and bake in the preheated oven for 30 minutes.

9. Remove foil and bake for an additional 10 minutes, or until cheese is melted and bubbly.

10. Garnish with chopped fresh parsley before serving.

Tips

Preparation: Prep ingredients ahead of time to streamline cooking.

Customization: Customize recipes with your favorite vegetables, proteins, or sauces.

Variations: Experiment with different herbs, spices, or additional ingredients to suit your taste preferences.

These dinner delights offer a range of flavors and textures, perfect for satisfying your family or guests any night of the week. Whether you opt for creamy pasta, flavorful stir-fry, or hearty casserole, these recipes are sure to become favorites at your dinner table.

Desserts to Impress: Cakes, Cookies, and Pies

When it comes to desserts that impress, cakes, cookies, and pies are timeless classics that never fail to delight. Here are recipes and tips to create each of these delicious treats:

Cakes

Classic Chocolate Cake:

Ingredients:

1 and 3/4 cups all-purpose flour

3/4 cup unsweetened cocoa powder

2 cups granulated sugar

1 and 1/2 teaspoons baking powder

1 and 1/2 teaspoons baking soda

1 teaspoon salt

2 large eggs

1 cup whole milk

1/2 cup vegetable oil

2 teaspoons vanilla extract

1 cup boiling water

Instructions:

1. Preheat your oven to 350°F (175°C). Grease and flour two 9-inch round cake pans.

2. In a large bowl, sift together flour, cocoa powder, sugar, baking powder, baking soda, and salt.

3. Add eggs, milk, oil, and vanilla extract to the dry ingredients. Beat on medium speed for 2 minutes.

4. Stir in boiling water (batter will be thin). Pour evenly into prepared pans.

5. Bake for 30 to 35 minutes in the preheated oven, until a toothpick inserted into the center comes out clean.

6. Cool in the pans for 10 minutes, then remove from pans and cool completely on a wire rack.

7. Frost with your favorite frosting (such as chocolate buttercream) and decorate as desired.

Cookies

Classic Chocolate Chip Cookies:

Ingredients:

1 cup unsalted butter, softened

3/4 cup granulated sugar

3/4 cup packed light brown sugar

1 teaspoon vanilla extract

2 large eggs

2 and 1/4 cups all-purpose flour

1 teaspoon baking soda

1/2 teaspoon salt

2 cups semi-sweet chocolate chips

Instructions:

1. Preheat your oven to 375°F (190°C). Line baking sheets with parchment paper.

2. In a large bowl, cream together butter, granulated sugar, and brown sugar until smooth.

3. Beat in vanilla extract and eggs, one at a time, until well blended.

4. Combine flour, baking soda, and salt; gradually stir into the creamed mixture.

5. Fold in chocolate chips with a wooden spoon or spatula.

6. Drop rounded tablespoons of dough onto prepared baking sheets, spacing them 2 inches apart.

7. Bake for 9 to 11 minutes in the preheated oven, until edges are golden brown.

8. Allow cookies to cool on baking sheet for 5 minutes before transferring to a wire rack to cool completely.

Pies

Classic Apple Pie:

Ingredients:

1 recipe for double-crust pie pastry

6 cups thinly sliced, peeled apples (such as Granny Smith or Honeycrisp)

3/4 cup granulated sugar

2 tablespoons all-purpose flour

1 teaspoon ground cinnamon

1/4 teaspoon ground nutmeg

1 tablespoon lemon juice

2 tablespoons unsalted butter, cut into small pieces

1 egg, beaten (for egg wash)

1 tablespoon granulated sugar (for sprinkling)

Instructions:

1. Preheat your oven to 425°F (220°C). Roll out half of the pie pastry and line a 9-inch pie dish with it.

2. In a large bowl, combine sliced apples, sugar, flour, cinnamon, nutmeg, and lemon juice. Toss until apples are evenly coated.

3. Transfer apple mixture into the prepared pie crust. Dot with butter pieces.

4. Roll out the remaining pie pastry and place over the filling. Trim, seal, and flute edges. Cut slits in the top crust to allow steam to escape.

5. Brush the top crust with beaten egg and sprinkle with 1 tablespoon of sugar.

6. Cover edges loosely with foil to prevent over-browning.

7. Bake in the preheated oven for 40 to 50 minutes, or until the crust is golden brown and the filling is bubbly.

8. Cool on a wire rack before serving.

Tips:

Presentation: Decorate cakes with frosting, sprinkles, or fresh fruit. Dust cookies with powdered sugar or drizzle with melted chocolate. Serve pies with a scoop of vanilla ice cream or whipped cream.

Storage: Cakes and pies can be stored at room temperature for a few days, while cookies can be kept in an airtight container. Pies can also be refrigerated.

Variations: Experiment with different flavors and additions to customize your desserts, such as adding nuts or spices to cookies, or incorporating different fruits into pies.

These dessert recipes are sure to impress your family and friends, whether you're celebrating a special occasion or simply indulging in a sweet treat after dinner. Enjoy the process of baking and sharing these delightful creations!

Vegetarian and Vegan Cooking

Vegetarian and vegan cooking opens up a world of delicious and nutritious possibilities using plant-based ingredients. Whether you're exploring these diets for health reasons, ethical concerns, or simply to diversify your culinary skills, here's a guide to help you create satisfying vegetarian and vegan dishes:

Vegetarian Cooking:

Vegetarian diets exclude meat, poultry, and fish, but may include dairy products and eggs.

Key Ingredients:

✓ **Proteins:** Beans (black beans, chickpeas, lentils), tofu, tempeh, quinoa, eggs, dairy products (cheese, yogurt).

✓ **Vegetables:** Leafy greens (spinach, kale), bell peppers, tomatoes, broccoli, zucchini, mushrooms, carrots.

✓ **Grains:** Brown rice, whole wheat pasta, barley, couscous, bulgur.

✓ **Fruits:** Berries, apples, citrus fruits, bananas, mangoes.

Sample Recipes:

Vegetarian Chili: Made with kidney beans, tomatoes, bell peppers, onions, and spices. Serve with rice or cornbread.

Caprese Salad: Fresh tomatoes, mozzarella cheese, and basil leaves, drizzled with balsamic glaze and olive oil.

Vegetarian Stir-fry: Tofu or tempeh with mixed vegetables (bell peppers, broccoli, carrots) in a savory sauce served over rice or noodles.

Vegan Cooking:

Vegan diets exclude all animal products, including meat, dairy, eggs, and honey.

Key Ingredients:

✓ **Proteins:** Beans, lentils, chickpeas, tofu, tempeh, quinoa, nuts (almonds, cashews, walnuts).

✓ **Vegetables:** Same as vegetarian, plus incorporate more leafy greens and cruciferous vegetables.

✓ **Grains:** Same as vegetarian, ensuring they're free from animal-based ingredients (like honey).

✓ **Fruits:** Same as vegetarian, with an emphasis on fresh and seasonal options.

Sample Recipes:

Vegan Buddha Bowl: Quinoa, roasted sweet potatoes, chickpeas, avocado slices, and a tahini dressing.

Vegan Pasta Primavera: Whole wheat pasta with sautéed vegetables (zucchini, cherry tomatoes, spinach) in a garlic and olive oil sauce.

Vegan Coconut Curry: Tofu or chickpeas cooked in a flavorful coconut milk curry sauce with vegetables (bell peppers, carrots, cauliflower), served over rice.

Tips for Vegetarian and Vegan Cooking:

Substitutions: Replace dairy milk with almond milk or soy milk. Use nutritional yeast for a cheesy flavor in vegan dishes. Substitute eggs with flaxseed meal or mashed bananas in baking.

Flavor Enhancement: Experiment with herbs, spices, and condiments (like soy sauce, miso paste, and tahini) to enhance flavors in plant-based dishes.

Nutritional Balance: Ensure your meals are well-balanced by including a variety of vegetables, proteins, grains, and fruits to meet your nutritional needs.

Explore Global Cuisine: Many cultures have rich traditions of vegetarian and vegan cooking (e.g., Indian, Mediterranean, Asian), offering a wide range of flavorful recipes to try.

Meal Planning: Plan ahead to ensure you have a variety of ingredients on hand. Batch-cooking grains, beans, and sauces can save time during busy weekdays.

Benefits of Vegetarian and Vegan Diets:

✓ **Health Benefits:** Lower risk of heart disease, hypertension, and certain cancers. Plant-based diets are often high in fiber, vitamins, and antioxidants.

✓ **Environmental Impact:** Reduced greenhouse gas emissions and conservation of water and land resources compared to animal agriculture.

✓ **Ethical Considerations:** Promotes compassion towards animals by avoiding their use in food production.

By exploring vegetarian and vegan cooking, you can discover new flavors and creative ways to enjoy meals that are both delicious and nutritious. Whether you're making a hearty vegan stew or a fresh vegetarian salad, these recipes and tips will help you create satisfying dishes that align with your dietary preferences and values.

Gluten-Free and Dairy-Free Options

Navigating a gluten-free and dairy-free diet requires careful consideration of ingredients and substitutions to ensure delicious and safe meals. Whether you have dietary restrictions or are exploring these options for health reasons, here's a guide to creating satisfying gluten-free and dairy-free dishes:

Gluten-Free Options

A gluten-free diet excludes wheat and related grains like barley, rye, and oats (unless certified gluten-free).

Key Ingredients:

✓ **Grains and Flours:** Rice, corn, quinoa, buckwheat, sorghum, millet, almond flour, coconut flour.

✓ **Starches:** Potato starch, tapioca starch, arrowroot starch.

✓ **Proteins:** Meat, poultry, fish, beans, legumes, tofu, tempeh.

✓ **Vegetables and Fruits:** All fresh and frozen fruits and vegetables are naturally gluten-free.

Sample Recipes:

Quinoa Salad: Quinoa with mixed vegetables (bell peppers, cucumber, cherry tomatoes) tossed in a lemon vinaigrette.

Grilled Chicken with Sweet Potato Mash: Marinated grilled chicken breasts served with mashed sweet potatoes and steamed green beans.

Stir-fried Tofu and Vegetables: Tofu stir-fried with broccoli, carrots, and snap peas in a gluten-free soy sauce.

Dairy-Free Options

A dairy-free diet excludes all dairy products, such as milk, cheese, yogurt, and butter.

Key Ingredients:

✓ **Milk Alternatives:** Almond milk, soy milk, coconut milk, oat milk, rice milk.

✓ **Butter Substitutes:** Coconut oil, olive oil, dairy-free margarine.

✓ **Cheese Alternatives:** Nut-based cheeses, nutritional yeast (for a cheesy flavor).

✓ **Yogurt Alternatives:** Coconut yogurt, almond yogurt, soy yogurt.

Sample Recipes:

Coconut Curry Lentil Soup: Red lentils cooked in a flavorful coconut milk broth with curry spices and vegetables (like carrots and spinach).

Vegan Pasta Alfredo: Gluten-free pasta tossed in a creamy sauce made from cashews, nutritional yeast, garlic, and almond milk.

Dairy-Free Chocolate Avocado Mousse: Avocado blended with cocoa powder, maple syrup, and almond milk for a creamy and decadent dessert.

Tips for Gluten-Free and Dairy-Free Cooking:

Read Labels: Be vigilant about checking food labels for gluten-containing ingredients (wheat, barley, rye) and dairy products (milk, cheese, butter).

Cross-Contamination: Prevent cross-contamination by using separate cooking utensils, cutting boards, and kitchen equipment for gluten-free and dairy-free preparations.

Experiment with Flavors: Use herbs, spices, and alternative ingredients (like coconut milk or nutritional yeast) to enhance flavors in dishes.

Baking Tips: Experiment with gluten-free flours (like almond flour or a gluten-free flour blend) and dairy-free substitutes (like applesauce or coconut yogurt) in baking recipes.

Explore Global Cuisines: Many cuisines naturally feature gluten-free and dairy-free dishes, such as Mediterranean, Asian, and Mexican cuisines.

Benefits of Gluten-Free and Dairy-Free Diets

◇ **Health Benefits:** Can alleviate symptoms of gluten intolerance (celiac disease) and lactose intolerance. May promote better digestion and overall well-being.

◇ **Expanded Culinary Horizons:** Encourages exploration of new ingredients and cooking techniques.

◇ **Allergen Management:** Essential for individuals with allergies or sensitivities to gluten or dairy.

By incorporating these tips and recipes into your cooking repertoire, you can create delicious and satisfying meals that cater to gluten-free and dairy-free dietary needs. Whether you're preparing a hearty stew, a creamy pasta dish, or a decadent dessert, these options ensure that everyone can enjoy flavorful and nutritious food.

Garnishing and Decorating Dishes

Garnishing and decorating dishes is not only about enhancing their visual appeal but also about adding complementary flavors and textures. Here's a guide to help you master the art of garnishing and decorating various types of dishes:

1. Types of Garnishes

Herbs and Greens:

Parsley: Fresh parsley leaves or chopped parsley add a vibrant green color and a hint of freshness to dishes.

Cilantro: Used in Latin American and Asian cuisines, cilantro adds a fresh, citrusy flavor.

Basil: Perfect for Italian dishes, basil leaves provide a sweet and aromatic touch.

Microgreens: Delicate and flavorful, microgreens like radish or pea shoots add a sophisticated touch to salads and main dishes.

Citrus Zest:

Lemon or Lime Zest: Grated zest from citrus fruits adds a burst of bright flavor and aroma to both sweet and savory dishes.

Orange Zest: Adds a slightly sweeter citrus flavor, ideal for desserts and savory dishes alike.

Nuts and Seeds:

Toasted Almonds: Add crunch and nuttiness to salads, vegetable dishes, or desserts.

Sesame Seeds: Sprinkle toasted sesame seeds over Asian dishes like stir-fries or noodle dishes.

Pumpkin Seeds: Provide texture and a hint of earthiness to soups, salads, and grain dishes.

Dairy and Dairy-Free Options:

Grated Cheese: Parmesan or pecorino cheese adds a savory umami flavor to pasta dishes and soups.

Coconut Flakes: Toasted coconut flakes add sweetness and crunch to desserts and breakfast dishes.

Edible Flowers:

Nasturtiums: Peppery flavor, great for garnishing salads or savory dishes.

Pansies: Mild flavor, suitable for decorating cakes, desserts, or salads.

Lavender: Fragrant and slightly sweet, ideal for infusing into syrups or garnishing desserts.

2. Tips for Garnishing and Decorating

Balance and Contrast: Choose garnishes that complement the flavors and textures of the dish. For example, a creamy soup might benefit from a sprinkle of crunchy toasted nuts.

Placement: Arrange garnishes strategically to enhance the presentation. For soups or sauces, place herbs or citrus zest in the center. For plated meals, scatter herbs or nuts around the main component.

Color Contrast: Use garnishes to add pops of color that contrast with the main dish. For example, bright green herbs stand out against a creamy pasta dish.

Texture: Consider texture when choosing garnishes. Crispy bacon bits can add a satisfying crunch to a creamy soup, while a dollop of whipped cream can soften the richness of a dessert.

Edible Garnishes: Ensure that garnishes are edible and add to the dish's flavor profile. Avoid using non-edible flowers or decorations that may contain toxins.

3. Decorating Desserts

Cakes:

Fresh Fruit: Berries, sliced kiwi, or mango add a burst of color and freshness to cake tops.

Chocolate Shavings: Use a vegetable peeler to create delicate chocolate curls or shavings for a luxurious touch.

Edible Flowers: Pansies or roses can be used to decorate cakes, providing an elegant and romantic flair.

Cookies and Bars:

Drizzles: Melted chocolate, caramel sauce, or icing drizzles can add visual appeal and extra sweetness.

Sprinkles: Colorful sprinkles or edible glitter can be sprinkled over icing or melted chocolate for a festive look.

Pies and Tarts:

Whipped Cream: Pipe rosettes or swirls of whipped cream around the edges of pies and tarts.

Fruit Arrangements: Arrange sliced fruit (like strawberries or kiwi) in a decorative pattern over the top of fruit tarts or pies.

4. Final Touches:

✓ **Practice Makes Perfect:** Experiment with different garnishes and decorations to find what works best for each dish.

✓ **Attention to Detail:** Pay attention to the final presentation, as it can elevate the dining experience and make the dish more appetizing.

✓ **Seasonal Inspiration:** Use seasonal ingredients and colors to inspire your garnishes and decorations, enhancing the dish's freshness and appeal.

Mastering the art of garnishing and decorating dishes not only enhances their visual appeal but also allows you to showcase your creativity and attention to detail in the kitchen. Whether you're garnishing a savory soup or decorating a decadent dessert, these tips and ideas will help you create beautiful and delicious dishes that impress.

Creating Memorable Dining Experiences

Creating memorable dining experiences goes beyond just serving delicious food; it involves crafting an atmosphere, engaging all senses, and focusing on the overall guest experience. Here are key elements to consider when aiming to create memorable dining experiences:

1. Ambiance and Atmosphere

✓ **Lighting:** Adjust lighting to set the mood—soft, dim lighting can create intimacy, while brighter lights are suitable for casual settings.

✓ **Music:** Choose background music that complements the dining experience—soft jazz for fine dining or upbeat tunes for a lively atmosphere.

✓ **Decor:** Table settings, floral arrangements, and decor should reflect the theme or style of the meal. Fresh flowers, candles, or themed centerpieces can enhance ambiance.

2. Hospitality and Service

✓ **Warm Welcome:** Greet guests with a friendly smile and genuine hospitality. Make them feel valued and comfortable from the moment they arrive.

✓ **Attentive Service:** Provide attentive but unobtrusive service. Anticipate needs and offer recommendations or assistance when necessary.

✓ **Personalization:** If possible, personalize the experience—remember guest preferences, celebrate special occasions, or offer customized menu options.

3. Menu and Food Presentation

✓ **Quality Ingredients:** Use fresh, seasonal ingredients prepared with care. Highlight local specialties or unique flavors to create a memorable culinary experience.

✓ **Creative Presentation:** Plate dishes thoughtfully with attention to color, texture, and arrangement. Garnish dishes appropriately to enhance visual appeal.

✓ **Tasting Menu or Pairings:** Offer tasting menus or wine pairings to allow guests to explore a variety of flavors and experience a curated culinary journey.

4. Engagement and Storytelling:

✓ **Chef Interaction:** If possible, offer opportunities for guests to interact with the chef—whether through an open kitchen concept or chef's table experience.

✓ **Menu Story:** Share stories behind dishes or ingredients—origins, culinary traditions, or chef inspirations—to enrich the dining experience.

✓ **Food Experiences:** Incorporate unique food experiences, such as live cooking stations, tableside preparations, or tasting flights, to engage guests.

5. Surprise and Delight:

✓ **Amuse-Bouche:** Start the meal with a small, complimentary appetizer or palate cleanser to surprise and set the tone for the dining experience.

✓ **Unexpected Treats:** Surprise guests with unexpected treats—a palate-cleansing sorbet between courses, a complimentary dessert, or a special beverage.

✓ **Parting Gift:** Send guests home with a memorable parting gift—such as house-made truffles, a recipe card, or a small memento related to the dining experience.

6. Feedback and Follow-Up:

✓ **Feedback Loop:** Encourage feedback from guests to understand their preferences and improve future experiences. Act on constructive feedback to enhance service and offerings.

✓ **Follow-Up:** Consider sending a thank-you note or email after the dining experience. Invite guests to return for special events or new menu launches.

7. Sustainability and Ethics:

✓ **Ethical Sourcing:** Highlight sustainable practices and ethical sourcing of ingredients. Share information about local suppliers or eco-friendly initiatives.

✓ **Community Engagement:** Support local community initiatives or charities. Engage guests in meaningful ways to contribute or participate in social responsibility efforts.

Conclusion

Creating memorable dining experiences requires attention to detail, creativity, and a genuine passion for hospitality. By focusing on ambiance, hospitality, culinary excellence, storytelling, surprise elements, and guest engagement, you can create dining experiences that leave a lasting impression. Whether it's a special occasion, a casual gathering, or a fine dining experience, each meal should be an opportunity to delight guests and create cherished memories.

Chapter 8: Presentation and Plating

Presentation and plating in the context of food refer to how a dish is visually arranged and served to enhance its appeal to the diner. Here are some key points to consider for effective presentation and plating:

Balance and Composition: The arrangement should be balanced both in terms of colors and textures. Use a combination of different colors (from ingredients and garnishes) to create visual interest. Avoid overcrowding the plate; leave some empty space for a clean look.

Use of Space: Consider the size of the plate and how the elements of the dish will fit together. Use negative space to your advantage to highlight the main components of the dish.

Height and Layers: Adding height to the dish can create a sense of elegance. This can be achieved through layering components or using garnishes that add verticality without overwhelming the plate.

Color Contrast: Colors should complement each other and the overall theme of the dish. Contrast can be achieved through the natural colors of ingredients or by adding vibrant garnishes.

Garnishes: Use garnishes sparingly and purposefully. They should enhance the dish's flavors and appearance without overpowering it. Fresh herbs, edible flowers, or sauces drizzled artistically can add a finishing touch.

Plate Shape and Size: The shape and size of the plate should be chosen based on the type of dish and the effect you want to achieve. Different shapes can create different visual impacts.

Cleanliness and Neatness: The plate should be clean and free of drips or smudges. Wipe the edges of the plate if needed before serving.

Theme and Style: Consider the overall theme or style of the cuisine or the occasion when plating. A formal dinner may call for a different presentation style compared to a casual brunch.

Temperature and Timing: Serve the dish at the appropriate temperature and ensure that hot items stay hot and cold items stay cold until they are served.

Practice and Experimentation: Plating is an art that improves with practice. Experiment with different arrangements and styles to find what works best for each dish.

Overall, presentation and plating should enhance the dining experience by appealing to both the eyes and the palate, making the meal more enjoyable and memorable.

Plate Presentation Techniques

Plate presentation techniques can greatly enhance the visual appeal of a dish. Here are some specific techniques and tips to consider:

Central Placement: Position the main item or protein of the dish in the center of the plate. This central focus helps draw the diner's eye to the most important component.

Layering: Create layers with different elements of the dish. For example, place vegetables or grains underneath the protein to add depth and interest.

Stacking: Stack components neatly to add height to the dish. For instance, layer slices of vegetables or arrange smaller items on top of each other.

Sweeping or Swirling Sauces: Use a spoon or squeeze bottle to create elegant swirls or drizzles of sauce on the plate. This adds artistic flair and enhances the dish's presentation.

Rim Decoration: Decorate the rim of the plate with complementary ingredients or garnishes. This frames the dish and adds a finishing touch to the presentation.

Color Contrast: Arrange ingredients with contrasting colors to create visual appeal. For example, pair bright vegetables with darker proteins or use colorful garnishes strategically.

Use of Negative Space: Leave some areas of the plate empty to allow the dish to breathe visually. This prevents overcrowding and helps focus attention on the main elements.

Garnishes and Accents: Use fresh herbs, microgreens, edible flowers, or citrus zest as garnishes. These add color, texture, and a pop of flavor while enhancing the overall presentation.

Precision and Cleanliness: Pay attention to the neatness and cleanliness of the plate. Wipe any spills or smudges carefully before serving to ensure a polished presentation.

Plate Shape and Size: Choose plates that complement the dish and allow its presentation to shine. Different shapes (round, square, rectangular) can create different visual effects.

Theme Consistency: Ensure that the presentation aligns with the theme or style of the cuisine. This includes considering cultural influences, seasonality, and the overall dining experience.

Practice and Experimentation: Don't be afraid to experiment with different plating techniques. Practice helps refine your skills and allows you to develop your own signature style.

By using these plate presentation techniques effectively, you can elevate the dining experience and make your dishes visually appealing and enticing to the diner.

Garnishing and Decorating Dishes

Garnishing and decorating dishes is an art form that enhances the presentation and appeal of food. Here are some tips and techniques for garnishing and decorating dishes effectively:

Purpose and Functionality: Garnishes should not only look appealing but also complement the flavors and textures of the dish. They can add contrasting flavors, textures, or colors that enhance the overall dining experience.

Types of Garnishes:

Fresh Herbs: Sprigs of parsley, cilantro, basil, or dill can add freshness and a pop of color.

Edible Flowers: Delicate flowers like pansies, nasturtiums, or orchids can be used to add a beautiful and elegant touch.

Citrus Zest: Grated or peeled zest from citrus fruits (lemon, lime, orange) adds brightness and a hint of citrus aroma.

Microgreens: Tiny greens like micro parsley, micro arugula, or micro radish can add a subtle crunch and visual interest.

Sauces and Drizzles: Use sauces or reductions to create artistic swirls or drizzles on the plate, enhancing both flavor and presentation.

Placement:

Place garnishes strategically to balance the plate visually. Avoid overcrowding or placing garnishes in a way that overwhelms the main components of the dish.

Consider using the rule of thirds or other compositional techniques to guide the placement of garnishes.

Color Contrast:

Choose garnishes that provide contrast with the colors of the dish. For example, a bright green herb garnish can stand out against a darker protein or sauce.

Use garnishes to highlight specific elements of the dish, such as placing a vibrant garnish near the focal point of the plate.

Edible Accessories:

Utilize edible accessories like crispy shallots, toasted nuts or seeds, or flavored oils to add texture and flavor.

Consider incorporating small, edible items that add a playful or thematic element to the dish, such as tiny herb-infused foam or vegetable crisps.

Creativity and Consistency:

Experiment with different garnishing techniques to develop your own style and flair.

Ensure that the garnishes align with the overall theme or style of the dish and the dining experience.

Practical Considerations:

Keep garnishes fresh and prepare them just before serving to maintain their vibrant colors and flavors.

Practice precision and attention to detail when placing garnishes to achieve a polished presentation.

By mastering the art of garnishing and decorating dishes, you can transform even simple dishes into visually stunning creations that delight both the eyes and the palate of your diners.

Creating Memorable Dining Experiences

Creating memorable dining experiences involves more than just serving delicious food. It's about crafting a holistic experience that engages all the senses and leaves a lasting impression on your guests. Here are key elements to consider:

Ambiance and Atmosphere:

Set the mood with appropriate lighting, music, and decor that aligns with the theme or style of your restaurant or event.

Consider the layout of the dining area to ensure comfort and privacy for diners.

Warm Welcome and Hospitality:

Greet guests warmly and make them feel valued from the moment they arrive.

Train staff to provide attentive, knowledgeable, and friendly service throughout the meal.

Thoughtful Menu Design:

Craft a menu that balances familiar favorites with innovative dishes that showcase your culinary expertise.

Consider offering tasting menus or themed experiences to provide variety and intrigue.

Presentation and Plating:

Pay attention to the visual presentation of each dish, using techniques like garnishing and artistic plating to enhance appeal.

Ensure consistency in portion sizes and quality across all servings.

Quality of Ingredients:

Source fresh, seasonal ingredients that are locally sourced whenever possible.

Highlight unique or specialty ingredients that add depth and interest to your dishes.

Interactive Elements:

Offer interactive experiences such as chef's tables, live cooking demonstrations, or customizable options that engage guests directly with the culinary process.

Pairings and Recommendations:

Provide knowledgeable wine or beverage pairings that complement the flavors of the food.

Offer guidance and recommendations on menu selections based on guest preferences.

Surprise and Delight:

Incorporate unexpected elements such as amuse-bouches, palate cleansers, or small gifts to create memorable moments throughout the meal.

Attention to Detail:

Ensure that every aspect of the dining experience, from table settings to restroom cleanliness, reflects a commitment to excellence.

Feedback and Follow-Up:

Solicit feedback from guests to continuously improve your offerings and service.

Follow up with personalized thank-you notes or offers to encourage return visits.

Consistency and Continuity:

Maintain high standards in all aspects of your restaurant or event to build a reputation for excellence over time.

Continuously innovate and evolve your offerings to keep guests excited and engaged.

By focusing on these elements, you can create dining experiences that are not only memorable but also build customer loyalty and positive word-of-mouth recommendations. Each detail contributes to the overall impression guests take away from their time with you, making dining more than just a meal but an unforgettable experience.

Common Cooking Mistakes and How to Fix Them

Cooking mistakes happen to everyone, but knowing how to identify and correct them can greatly improve your culinary skills. Here are some common cooking mistakes and solutions to fix them:

1. Overcooking or Burning Food:

Mistake: Leaving food unattended or cooking at too high a temperature can lead to overcooked or burnt dishes.

Solution:

✓ **Monitor Heat:** Adjust heat settings as needed and keep an eye on cooking times. Use a timer if necessary to prevent overcooking.

✓ **Stir Regularly:** Stirring prevents food from sticking and burning on the bottom of the pan.

✓ **Use a Lid:** Covering pans while cooking can help retain moisture and prevent burning, especially for meats and vegetables.

2. Under Seasoning or Over Seasoning:

Mistake: Not adding enough seasoning results in bland dishes, while over seasoning can overpower flavors.

Solution:

✓ **Taste as You Go:** Taste your food during cooking and adjust seasoning gradually. Remember, you can always add more seasoning but can't take it away.

✓ **Layer Flavors:** Use a combination of herbs, spices, and aromatics to build depth of flavor without relying solely on salt.

✓ **Balance Salt:** If a dish becomes too salty, add acidity (like lemon juice or vinegar) or sweetness (like a pinch of sugar) to balance flavors.

3. Tough Meat:

Mistake: Cooking meat at too high a temperature or for too long can make it tough and dry.

Solution:

✓ **Low and Slow:** For tougher cuts of meat, use low heat over a longer period (braising or slow cooking) to tenderize.

✓ **Resting Time:** Let cooked meat rest before slicing to allow juices to redistribute and keep it moist.

✓ **Marinating:** Marinate meat beforehand with acidic ingredients (like vinegar or citrus juice) to tenderize it before cooking.

4. Soggy Vegetables:

Mistake: Overcooking vegetables or overcrowding the pan can result in soggy, mushy vegetables.

Solution:

✓ **Quick Cooking:** Use high heat and cook vegetables quickly to retain their crunch and vibrant color.

✓ **Steaming or Roasting:** Steam or roast vegetables instead of boiling to preserve their texture and flavor.

✓ **Shock in Ice Water:** If blanching vegetables, shock them in ice water immediately after boiling to stop cooking and retain crispness.

5. Sticky Rice or Pasta:

Mistake: Not rinsing rice before cooking or overcooking pasta can lead to sticky, clumpy grains.

Solution:

✓ **Rinse Rice:** Rinse rice under cold water until the water runs clear before cooking to remove excess starch.

✓ **Use Enough Water:** Cook pasta in a large pot of boiling, salted water with plenty of space to move around.

✓ **Stir Pasta:** Stir pasta occasionally while cooking to prevent sticking. Add a bit of olive oil after draining to keep pasta loose.

6. Curdled Sauces or Custards:

Mistake: Heating dairy products too quickly or not tempering eggs properly can cause sauces or custards to curdle.

Solution:

✓ **Temper Eggs:** Gradually add a small amount of hot liquid to beaten eggs while whisking constantly before adding them back to the hot mixture.

✓ **Low Heat:** Heat dairy-based sauces or custards over low to medium heat, stirring constantly, to avoid curdling.

✓ **Cornstarch Slurry:** For thinner sauces, mix cornstarch with cold water and add it to the sauce to thicken without curdling.

7. Dense Baked Goods:

Mistake: Overmixing batter or using expired leavening agents (like baking powder or yeast) can result in dense, heavy baked goods.

Solution:

✓ **Mix Gently:** Mix dry and wet ingredients just until combined. Overmixing activates gluten, making baked goods dense.

✓ **Fresh Leavening Agents:** Ensure baking powder, baking soda, or yeast are fresh and active before using.

✓ **Room Temperature Ingredients:** Use room temperature eggs and butter for better incorporation and lighter texture in cakes and cookies.

8. Uneven Cooking:

Mistake: Placing food unevenly on the pan or overcrowding the oven can lead to uneven cooking.

Solution:

✓ **Even Placement:** Arrange food evenly on the cooking surface or tray to ensure even cooking.

✓ **Rotate or Flip:** Rotate pans halfway through cooking or flip food (like burgers or chicken breasts) to cook evenly on both sides.

✓ **Use Oven Racks:** Use multiple oven racks and rotate dishes if necessary to ensure even heat distribution.

9. Forgetting to Preheat:

Mistake: Adding food to a cold pan or oven can affect cooking times and result in unevenly cooked dishes.

Solution:

✓ **Preheat Properly:** Preheat your oven or pan according to the recipe instructions before adding food.

✓ **Use a Thermometer:** Use an oven thermometer to ensure accurate temperature readings, especially if your oven tends to run hot or cold.

10. Not Following Recipes:

Mistake: Not following recipes accurately can lead to unexpected results or flavors.

Solution:

✓ **Read Before Starting:** Read the entire recipe before beginning to ensure you have all ingredients and equipment ready.

✓ **Measure Ingredients:** Use measuring cups and spoons for accuracy, especially for baking.

✓ **Adjust as Needed:** If you need to substitute ingredients, research proper equivalents or adjustments to maintain consistency.

Conclusion:

By recognizing common cooking mistakes and knowing how to fix them, you can improve your cooking skills and create more delicious and enjoyable meals. Practice and experimentation will also help you gain confidence in the kitchen, ensuring that your dishes turn out well and impress your family and guests.

Time-Saving Techniques in the Kitchen

Time-saving techniques in the kitchen can streamline meal preparation, making cooking more efficient and enjoyable. Here are some effective strategies to save time while cooking:

1. Meal Planning:

Plan Ahead: Spend time each week planning meals and creating a shopping list. This reduces last-minute trips to the grocery store and ensures you have all ingredients on hand.

Batch Cooking: Prepare larger quantities of meals that freeze well, such as soups, stews, or casseroles. Freeze individual portions for quick and easy meals later.

2. Organization and Preparation:

Prep Ingredients: Wash, peel, chop, and measure ingredients in advance. Store them in containers or zip-top bags in the refrigerator until ready to use.

Mise en Place: Set up your workspace with all necessary tools and ingredients before starting to cook. This prevents interruptions and keeps cooking organized.

3. Cooking Techniques:

One-Pot Meals: Prepare meals that cook all components in a single pot or pan, minimizing cleanup and cooking time.

Pressure Cooker or Instant Pot: Use these appliances for faster cooking times, especially for dishes like stews, grains, and beans.

Sheet Pan Meals: Roast meats and vegetables together on a sheet pan for easy cleanup and minimal hands-on cooking.

4. Kitchen Tools and Gadgets:

Food Processor or Blender: Use these for chopping vegetables, making sauces, or blending ingredients quickly.

Slow Cooker: Set up ingredients in the morning for a meal that cooks slowly throughout the day, requiring minimal attention.

Microwave: Utilize for reheating leftovers or quickly cooking certain vegetables.

5. Cleanup:

Clean as You Go: Wash utensils, cutting boards, and other tools while cooking to keep your workspace organized.

Dishwasher Use: Load dirty dishes into the dishwasher immediately after use to avoid buildup and make cleanup faster.

Dispose of Waste: Use a compost bin or garbage bowl near your workspace for easy disposal of food scraps and packaging.

6. Time-Saving Tips:

Use Frozen Ingredients: Frozen fruits, vegetables, and proteins can be quickly incorporated into meals without the need for chopping or prepping.

Store-Bought Shortcuts: Utilize pre-cut vegetables, canned beans, or cooked grains to cut down on prep time.

Multi-Tasking: Coordinate tasks to maximize efficiency, such as boiling pasta while preparing a sauce or dressing.

7. Efficiency Mindset:

Practice and Experience: With practice, you'll become more efficient at meal preparation and cooking techniques.

Simplify Recipes: Choose recipes with fewer ingredients or simpler instructions to save time without sacrificing flavor.

By incorporating these time-saving techniques into your cooking routine, you can minimize stress, save valuable time, and enjoy delicious meals more easily. Whether you're preparing weekday dinners or hosting a gathering, these strategies will help streamline your kitchen tasks and make cooking a more enjoyable experience.

Advice from Professional Chefs

Drawing on insights from professional chefs, here are some valuable pieces of advice that can elevate your cooking skills and enhance your experience in the kitchen:

1. Start with Quality Ingredients:

Chef's Insight: "The quality of your ingredients will always dictate the outcome of your dish."

> **Advice:** Invest in fresh, seasonal produce, meats, and pantry staples. Look for local ingredients, when possible, as they often offer superior flavor and freshness.

2. Master Basic Techniques:

Chef's Insight: "Mastering basic techniques forms the foundation for all great cooking."

> **Advice:** Focus on knife skills, sautéing, roasting, and basic sauces. Practice these techniques regularly to build confidence and efficiency in the kitchen.

3. Mise en Place (Everything in its Place):

Chef's Insight: "Organize your workspace and prep ingredients before you start cooking."

> **Advice:** Set up all tools and ingredients (mise en place) before cooking. This reduces stress, prevents mistakes, and allows you to focus on cooking techniques and flavor development.

4. Taste and Adjust:

Chef's Insight: "Taste your food throughout the cooking process and adjust seasoning as needed."

> **Advice:** Season dishes gradually and taste as you go. This ensures balanced flavors and prevents over-seasoning. Remember, you can always add more seasoning but can't take it away.

5. Attention to Detail:

Chef's Insight: "Pay attention to every detail, from plating to final touches."

Advice: Presentation matters. Take care in plating your dishes attractively, considering colors, textures, and garnishes. This enhances the dining experience and showcases your culinary skills.

6. Practice and Experiment:

Chef's Insight: "Cooking is a journey of continuous learning and discovery."

Advice: Don't be afraid to experiment with new ingredients, flavors, and techniques. Embrace failures as learning opportunities and keep refining your skills through practice.

7. Clean as You Go:

Chef's Insight: "A clean kitchen is essential for efficient cooking."

Advice: Wash utensils, cutting boards, and countertops as you cook to maintain order and prevent clutter. This makes cleanup easier and allows you to focus on cooking.

8. Respect Ingredients and Techniques:

Chef's Insight: "Respect the ingredients you work with and the techniques you employ."

Advice: Learn about the origins and characteristics of ingredients. Use appropriate cooking methods to highlight their natural flavors and textures.

9. Embrace Creativity:

Chef's Insight: "Cooking is an art form; let your creativity shine."

Advice: Don't be afraid to think outside the box and create unique flavor combinations. Trust your instincts and explore different culinary styles and cuisines.

10. Enjoy the Process:

Chef's Insight: "Cooking should be enjoyable and rewarding."

Advice: Have fun in the kitchen! Enjoy the process of cooking, sharing meals with loved ones, and celebrating the flavors and traditions of food.

Conclusion

By incorporating these insights and advice from professional chefs into your cooking journey, you can enhance your skills, elevate your dishes, and gain a deeper appreciation for the art of cooking. Whether you're a beginner or seasoned home cook, these principles will guide you toward creating delicious and memorable meals for yourself and others.

Exploring Advanced Techniques

Exploring advanced cooking techniques can be both rewarding and challenging, allowing you to elevate your culinary skills and create impressive dishes. Here are several advanced techniques that chefs often use, along with tips on how to approach them:

1. Sous Vide Cooking:

Overview: Sous vide involves cooking vacuum-sealed ingredients in a water bath at precise temperatures for extended periods.

Tips:

Equipment: Invest in a sous vide immersion circulator for precise temperature control.

Preparation: Season ingredients and vacuum-seal them before cooking for enhanced flavor infusion.

Finish: Sear meats or vegetables post sous vide to develop a caramelized exterior for added texture and flavor.

2. Molecular Gastronomy:

Overview: Molecular gastronomy explores scientific principles to transform food textures and presentations.

Tips:

Ingredients: Experiment with hydrocolloids (like agar-agar or xanthan gum) and emulsifiers (like lecithin) to create unique textures.

Techniques: Use spherification to create spheres or gels, and foams using whipping siphons for airy textures.

Presentation: Focus on visual aesthetics by using edible foams, encapsulations, or deconstructions of traditional dishes.

3. Precision Baking:

Overview: Precision baking requires exact measurements and techniques for consistent and delicate desserts.

Tips:

Measurements: Use digital scales and precise measuring tools for accuracy.

Techniques: Master tempering chocolate, making laminated doughs (like croissants), and creating intricate cake decorations.

Ingredients: Understand the chemistry of baking (like gluten development and leavening agents) for precise control over texture and rise.

4. Advanced Knife Skills:

Overview: Advanced knife skills involve precise cutting techniques for professional presentation and even cooking.

Tips:

Techniques: Practice julienning, brunoise, and chiffonade cuts for uniformity and aesthetic appeal.

Safety: Focus on proper grip and hand positioning to avoid accidents and increase efficiency.

Maintenance: Keep knives sharp with regular honing and sharpening to maintain cutting precision.

5. Fermentation and Preservation:

Overview: Fermentation and preservation techniques enhance flavors and prolong shelf life through natural processes.

Tips:

Ingredients: Experiment with fermenting vegetables (like kimchi or sauerkraut) and dairy (like yogurt or cheese) for complex flavors.

Techniques: Master curing meats, smoking fish, and pickling fruits for unique preservation methods.

Safety: Understand food safety protocols to prevent contamination during fermentation and preservation processes.

6. Advanced Sauce Making:

Overview: Advanced sauce making involves mastering reduction, emulsion, and balancing flavors for sophisticated dishes.

Tips:

Reduction: Practice reducing stocks and liquids to concentrate flavors and thicken sauces.

Emulsion: Learn to create stable emulsions (like hollandaise or mayonnaise) by slowly incorporating fats into liquids.

Flavor Balancing: Experiment with acidity (like vinegar or citrus), sweetness (like honey or caramelization), and umami (like soy sauce or mushrooms) for depth of flavor.

7. Plating and Presentation:

Overview: Plating and presentation techniques transform dishes into visual masterpieces that enhance the dining experience.

Tips:

Composition: Use negative space and geometric shapes to create balance and focus on the plate.

Color and Texture: Incorporate vibrant colors and contrasting textures (like crunchy garnishes or creamy sauces) for visual interest.

Garnishes: Employ edible flowers, microgreens, or delicate sauces to add complexity and elevate the overall presentation.

8. Regional and Ethnic Cuisine:

Overview: Explore regional and ethnic cuisines to expand your culinary repertoire and incorporate authentic flavors.

Tips:

Research: Study traditional recipes and cooking methods from diverse cultures.

Ingredients: Source authentic spices, herbs, and specialty ingredients to capture authentic flavors.

Techniques: Practice traditional cooking techniques (like tandoor grilling, wok frying, or tagine cooking) for authenticity and depth of flavor.

9. Foraging and Wild Ingredients:

Overview: Foraging introduces wild ingredients into culinary creations, emphasizing sustainability and unique flavors.

Tips:

Identification: Learn to identify edible wild plants, mushrooms, and herbs in your region.

Harvesting: Harvest responsibly and ethically, respecting natural habitats and regulations.

Integration: Incorporate foraged ingredients into dishes to highlight their natural flavors and seasonal availability.

10. Continuing Education and Practice:

Overview: Advanced techniques require ongoing learning, practice, and experimentation to refine skills and develop personal style.

Tips:

Courses and Workshops: Attend culinary classes, workshops, or seminars to learn from experts and gain hands-on experience.

Practice: Dedicate time to practice new techniques regularly to build proficiency and confidence in the kitchen.

Feedback: Seek feedback from peers, chefs, or mentors to refine techniques and improve culinary outcomes.

Conclusion:

Exploring advanced cooking techniques involves curiosity, patience, and a commitment to continuous learning. By mastering these techniques and incorporating them into your cooking repertoire, you can elevate your culinary skills, create impressive dishes, and delight family and guests with memorable dining experiences.

Resources for Further Learning

If you're eager to expand your culinary skills and knowledge, there are numerous resources available to help you learn and grow in the kitchen. Here's a curated list of valuable resources for further learning:

1. Online Cooking Courses and Classes

Masterclass: Offers courses taught by world-renowned chefs like Gordon Ramsay, Thomas Keller, and Massimo Bottura, covering various cuisines and techniques.

Coursera: Provides online courses in culinary arts, food science, and nutrition from universities and culinary schools worldwide.

Udemy: Offers a wide range of cooking classes on topics from basic techniques to advanced cuisines, often at affordable prices.

Skill Share: Features cooking and baking classes taught by professionals, focusing on specific techniques, recipes, and kitchen skills.

2. Cooking Websites and Blogs

Serious Eats: Provides in-depth articles, recipes, and technique tutorials from a team of culinary experts.

Bon Appétit: Offers a variety of recipes, cooking tips, and video tutorials from chefs and food enthusiasts.

Food52: Curates recipes, cooking advice, and community discussions on food and cooking trends.

The Kitchn: Offers practical cooking tips, meal planning guides, and kitchen product reviews.

3. Cookbooks and Reference Books

The Joy of Cooking by Irma S. Rombauer: A comprehensive guide covering everything from basic recipes to advanced techniques.

On Food and Cooking: The Science and Lore of the Kitchen by Harold McGee: Explores the science behind cooking techniques and ingredients.

Modernist Cuisine: The Art and Science of Cooking by Nathan Myhrvold: A detailed exploration of modern cooking techniques and equipment.

The Flavor Bible by Karen Page and Andrew Dornenburg: A guide to pairing flavors and ingredients to create harmonious dishes.

4. Culinary Schools and Workshops

Culinary Institute of America (CIA): Offers professional culinary education programs and online courses for home cooks.

Le Cordon Bleu: Provides culinary arts training and workshops at locations worldwide.

Local Cooking Classes: Many community centers, culinary schools, and gourmet stores offer hands-on cooking classes for various skill levels.

5. YouTube Channels and Cooking Shows

Chef Steps: Features videos on advanced cooking techniques, sous vide, and modernist cuisine.

Binging with Babish: Recreates dishes from movies and TV shows, with a focus on technique and creativity.

America's Test Kitchen: Offers cooking tutorials, equipment reviews, and recipe testing from the editors of Cook's Illustrated.

Jamie Oliver's Food Tube: Jamie Oliver and other chefs share recipes, cooking tips, and kitchen hacks.

6. Food and Cooking Podcasts

The Splendid Table: Explores food culture, recipes, and interviews with chefs and food experts.

Bon Appétit Foodcast: Features discussions on cooking techniques, recipes, and culinary trends.

The Kitchen Counter: Offers practical cooking advice, tips, and interviews with chefs and cookbook authors.

7. Online Forums and Communities

Reddit: Subreddits like r/Cooking, r/AskCulinary, and r/recipes offer discussions, tips, and advice from a community of home cooks and professionals.

Chef Talk: A forum for chefs and culinary enthusiasts to discuss techniques, recipes, and industry news.

Food52 Hotline: Allows users to ask cooking questions and receive advice from the Food52 community.

8. Specialty Culinary Apps

Paprika: Helps organize recipes, create meal plans, and generate shopping lists.

Yummly: Provides personalized recipe recommendations based on dietary preferences and cooking skill level.

Cookpad: Allows users to share recipes, cooking tips, and photos with a global community of home cooks.

9. Social Media and Instagram

Chefs and Food Influencers: Follow chefs, food bloggers, and influencers on Instagram for recipe ideas, cooking demonstrations, and kitchen tips.

Hashtags: Explore popular food and cooking hashtags (#foodie, #instafood, #cookingtips) for inspiration and community engagement.

10. Local Food Events and Farmers Markets

Food Festivals: Attend local food festivals and culinary events to discover new ingredients, cooking techniques, and regional cuisines.

Farmers Markets: Connect with local farmers and artisans to learn about seasonal ingredients and cooking methods.

Whether you prefer hands-on classes, online resources, cookbooks, or social media, these resources offer diverse opportunities to expand your culinary knowledge and skills. Choose the platforms and formats that resonate most with your learning style and culinary interests, and enjoy your journey towards becoming a more skilled and confident cook.

Embracing Cooking as a Lifestyle

Embracing cooking as a lifestyle goes beyond simply preparing meals—it involves cultivating a deep appreciation for food, creativity in the kitchen, and a commitment to nourishing yourself and others. Here are some key aspects of embracing cooking as a lifestyle:

1. Developing a Connection with Food

Mindful Eating: Embrace the practice of mindful eating by savoring flavors, textures, and aromas of your meals.

Understanding Ingredients: Learn about different ingredients, their origins, and how they contribute to dishes.

Seasonal Cooking: Use seasonal produce to enhance flavors and support local agriculture.

2. Cultivating Creativity

Recipe Exploration: Experiment with new recipes, ingredients, and cooking techniques to expand your culinary repertoire.

Personalizing Dishes: Adapt recipes to suit your tastes, dietary preferences, and cultural influences.

Presentation: Focus on plating and presentation to elevate dining experiences at home.

3. Prioritizing Health and Nutrition

Balanced Meals: Plan meals that include a variety of nutrients, colors, and textures to support overall health.

Home Cooking vs. Processed Foods: Choose homemade dishes over processed foods to control ingredients and reduce added sugars, salts, and preservatives.

Special Diets: Accommodate dietary restrictions or preferences with thoughtful ingredient substitutions and creative alternatives.

4. Building Kitchen Skills

Learning Techniques: Master fundamental cooking techniques such as chopping, sautéing, roasting, and baking.

Advanced Skills: Challenge yourself with advanced techniques like sous vide cooking, pastry making, or fermenting.

Knife Skills: Hone your knife skills to improve efficiency and precision in the kitchen.

5. Creating Rituals and Traditions

Family Meals: Foster connections with loved ones through shared meals and cooking together.

Celebrations: Mark special occasions with homemade dishes and culinary traditions that hold personal or cultural significance.

Meal Planning: Develop meal planning routines to streamline grocery shopping and cooking throughout the week.

6. Embracing Sustainability

Food Waste Reduction: Minimize food waste by using leftovers creatively, preserving ingredients, and composting organic waste.

Sustainable Sourcing: Support local farmers and producers, choose ethically sourced ingredients, and consider the environmental impact of food choices.

Plant-Based Cooking: Incorporate more plant-based meals to reduce your carbon footprint and promote sustainable eating habits.

7. Community and Sharing

Sharing Recipes: Share recipes, cooking tips, and experiences with friends, family, and online communities.

Hosting Gatherings: Host dinner parties, potlucks, or cooking workshops to celebrate food and connect with others.

Supporting Local Food Initiatives: Engage with food-related events, farmers markets, and community-supported agriculture (CSA) programs.

8. Continuous Learning and Growth

Exploring Culinary Culture: Explore diverse cuisines, culinary traditions, and global flavors through travel, cooking classes, or cultural events.

Learning Resources: Utilize cookbooks, online courses, cooking shows, and culinary workshops to expand your knowledge and skills.

Adapting to Trends: Stay informed about food trends, nutrition research, and innovative cooking techniques to stay inspired and informed.

9. Mindful Cooking Practices

Stress Relief: Use cooking as a creative outlet and a way to unwind from daily stresses.

Time Management: Develop efficient meal preparation strategies and time-saving techniques to integrate cooking into a busy lifestyle.

Self-Care: Prioritize self-care through nourishing meals that promote physical well-being and mental clarity.

10. Celebrating Food as a Source of Joy

Gratitude: Cultivate gratitude for the ingredients, flavors, and experiences that cooking brings into your life.

Enjoyment: Find joy in the process of cooking, from meal planning and shopping to preparation and sharing meals with others.

Personal Growth: Reflect on how cooking enhances your life and fosters personal growth in creativity, patience, and culinary expertise.

By embracing cooking as a lifestyle, you can cultivate a deeper connection to food, enhance your culinary skills, and create meaningful experiences that nourish both body and soul. Whether you're a novice cook or seasoned chef, the journey of embracing cooking as a lifestyle is rich with opportunities for learning, creativity, and enjoyment.

Appendix

Measurement Conversion Charts

Measurement conversion charts are incredibly useful in the kitchen, especially when following recipes from different sources that use different units of measurement. Here are some common measurement conversion charts for cooking:

Volume Conversions:

Cups to Milliliters and Fluid Ounces:

1 cup = 237 ml = 8 fl oz

3/4 cup = 177 ml = 6 fl oz

1/2 cup = 118 ml = 4 fl oz

1/4 cup = 59 ml = 2 fl oz

1 tablespoon (tbsp) = 15 ml

1 teaspoon (tsp) = 5 ml

Liters to Quarts and Gallons:

1 liter (L) = 1.06 quarts (qt) = 0.26 gallons (gal)

1 quart (qt) = 0.95 liters = 0.25 gallons

1 gallon (gal) = 3.79 liters = 4 quarts

Weight Conversions

Ounces to Grams:

1 ounce (oz) = 28.35 grams (g)

8 oz = 227 g

4 oz = 113 g

2 oz = 57 g

1 oz = 28 g

Pounds to Kilograms:

1 pound (lb) = 0.45 kilograms (kg)

2 lb = 0.91 kg

3 lb = 1.36 kg

4 lb = 1.81 kg

Temperature Conversions

Fahrenheit to Celsius:

(°F - 32) / 1.8 = °C

350°F = 177°C

300°F = 149°C

250°F = 121°C

200°F = 93°C

Celsius to Fahrenheit:

(°C × 1.8) + 32 = °F

100°C = 212°F

75°C = 167°F

50°C = 122°F

25°C = 77°F

Oven Temperature Conversions

Gas Mark:

Gas Mark 1 = 275°F = 135°C

Gas Mark 2 = 300°F = 150°C

Gas Mark 3 = 325°F = 165°C

Gas Mark 4 = 350°F = 180°C

Gas Mark 5 = 375°F = 190°C

Additional Conversions

Dry Measurements:

1 cup all-purpose flour = 120 grams

1 cup granulated sugar = 200 grams

1 cup brown sugar = 220 grams

Butter Conversions:

1 stick of butter = 1/2 cup = 113 grams

1 tablespoon of butter = 14 grams

These conversion charts are essential for accurately measuring ingredients and ensuring successful cooking outcomes. Keep them handy in your kitchen or bookmark this page for quick reference!

Ingredient Substitution Guide

An ingredient substitution guide is invaluable in the kitchen when you're missing a key ingredient or need to accommodate dietary restrictions. Here's a comprehensive guide to common ingredient substitutions:

Baking Substitutions

Flour:

All-Purpose Flour: Whole wheat flour (with adjustments), bread flour, cake flour.

Gluten-Free: Almond flour, coconut flour, gluten-free flour blends.

Sugar:

Granulated Sugar: Brown sugar (increase moisture), honey, maple syrup.

Brown Sugar: Granulated sugar with molasses (1 cup sugar + 1 tbsp molasses).

Butter:

Unsalted Butter: Margarine, vegetable shortening, coconut oil (in some recipes).

Dairy-Free: Vegan butter, coconut oil, applesauce (for moisture).

Eggs:

Whole Eggs: Applesauce, mashed banana, yogurt, silken tofu (for binding).

Vegan: Flaxseed meal (1 tbsp ground flaxseed + 3 tbsp water per egg), chia seeds.

Milk:

Whole Milk: Skim milk, almond milk, soy milk, oat milk.

Buttermilk: Mix 1 cup milk with 1 tbsp vinegar or lemon juice, let stand for 5 minutes.

Leavening Agents:

Baking Powder: 1 part baking soda + 2 parts cream of tartar (for 1 tsp baking powder).

Baking Soda: 1/4 tsp baking soda + 1/2 tsp cream of tartar (for 1 tsp baking powder).

Cooking Substitutions

Oil:

Vegetable Oil: Canola oil, sunflower oil, olive oil (for sautéing).

High-Heat Cooking: Grapeseed oil, avocado oil.

Salt:

Table Salt: Kosher salt (use less due to coarser texture), sea salt.

Low Sodium: Herb blends, lemon juice, vinegar (for flavor).

Herbs and Spices:

Fresh Herbs: Dried herbs (use 1/3 of the amount), herb blends.

Spices: Cinnamon for nutmeg, paprika for chili powder (adjust to taste).

Stocks and Broths:

Chicken Broth: Vegetable broth, mushroom broth (for vegetarian options).

Beef Broth: Mushroom broth, vegetable broth.

Wine and Alcohol:

White Wine: Chicken or vegetable broth with lemon juice.

Red Wine: Beef or vegetable broth with vinegar.

Dietary and Allergy-Friendly Substitutions:

Gluten-Free:

Flour: Gluten-free flour blends, almond flour, coconut flour.

Thickener: Arrowroot starch, cornstarch (for sauces and gravies).

Dairy-Free:

Milk: Almond milk, soy milk, oat milk, coconut milk.

Cheese: Nutritional yeast, dairy-free cheese alternatives.

Vegan:

Eggs: Tofu (silken or firm), mashed banana, applesauce.

Butter: Vegan butter, coconut oil, olive oil.

Nut-Free:

Flour: Wheat flour, oat flour, rice flour.

Milk: Soy milk, oat milk, hemp milk.

Soy-Free:

Milk: Almond milk, oat milk, coconut milk.

Tofu: Chickpea flour, seitan, tempeh.

Tips for Substitutions

Proportion Adjustments: When substituting, consider texture, moisture, and flavor impacts on your dish.

Taste Testing: Always taste-test after substituting to adjust seasoning and flavors as needed.

Allergies and Restrictions: Verify ingredients for hidden allergens if substituting for dietary restrictions.

Recipe Suitability: Not all substitutions work universally; choose substitutions that complement the recipe's overall flavor profile and texture requirements.

By using this ingredient substitution guide, you can confidently adapt recipes to suit dietary needs, ingredient availability, or personal preferences without compromising on taste or quality in your cooking and baking endeavors.

Glossary of Cooking Terms

A glossary of cooking terms is essential for navigating recipes and understanding culinary techniques. Here's a comprehensive list of common cooking terms and their definitions:

A

Al dente: Italian term meaning "to the tooth"; refers to pasta or vegetables cooked until just firm when bitten.

Au gratin: Topped with breadcrumbs or cheese and browned in the oven or under a broiler.

B

Baste: To spoon or pour drippings, marinade, or fat over food (especially meat) during cooking to keep it moist.

Blanch: To briefly cook food in boiling water, then plunge into ice water to stop the cooking process; often used for vegetables or fruits to retain color and texture.

Braise: To cook food slowly in a closed vessel with a small amount of liquid, typically in the oven or on the stove, until tender.

C

Caramelize: To heat sugar until it liquefies and becomes a caramel color; also refers to cooking vegetables until natural sugars brown and become flavorful.

Chop: To cut food into small, irregular pieces.

Cream: To beat ingredients (usually butter and sugar) together until soft and fluffy.

D

Deglaze: To add liquid (such as wine, broth, or water) to a pan in which food, especially meat, has been cooked and stir to loosen browned bits stuck to the pan, which adds flavor to the dish.

Dice: To cut food into small, even cubes.

Dredge: To lightly coat food with flour, breadcrumbs, or cornmeal before cooking.

E

Emulsify: To blend together ingredients that don't normally mix well (like oil and vinegar) into a smooth, uniform mixture.

F

Fold: To gently combine ingredients (like whipped cream into a batter) with a spatula using a gentle up-and-over motion to avoid deflating the mixture.

Fry: To cook food in hot fat or oil until crisp and brown.

G

Grate: To shred food into small pieces using a grater.

Grill: To cook food on a grill over direct heat.

J

Julienne: To cut food into thin, matchstick-sized strips.

K

Knead: To work dough with the hands to develop gluten and create a smooth, elastic texture.

M

Marinate: To soak food in a mixture of ingredients (marinade) to add flavor and tenderize before cooking.

Mince: To cut food into very small pieces, smaller than chopped.

P

Poach: To cook food gently in liquid just below boiling point, often used for delicate items like eggs or fish.

Puree: To blend food until smooth and creamy, usually in a blender or food processor.

R

Reduce: To simmer a liquid (like sauce or stock) until it thickens and reduces in volume, intensifying flavors.

S

Sauté: To cook food quickly in a small amount of fat over high heat, stirring or tossing frequently.

Simmer: To cook food gently in liquid at a temperature just below boiling.

T

Toast: To cook food (like bread or nuts) until browned and crisp using dry heat.

W

Whisk: To beat ingredients vigorously with a whisk to incorporate air and achieve a smooth consistency.

Z

Zest: The outer, colorful part of citrus fruit peel used to add flavor to dishes.

Conclusion:

This glossary of cooking terms provides a foundation for understanding culinary techniques and instructions in recipes. Whether you're a beginner or seasoned cook, knowing these terms will help you navigate the kitchen with confidence and achieve delicious results in your cooking adventures.